Trans Voice

Trans Voice

A Collection of Prose Poems
of Transitioning
Gender, Spirit, and Life

Billie Sage

Trans Voice

First Edition

ISBN: 978-1974408382

To Matt

ACKNOWLEDGEMENTS

I would like to thank all the beautiful souls that have helped me transition through life, both in body and spirit. Many travel the stars now and many still give love and guidance every day.

I would like to especially thank the artists that have given their visual art to me to enhance the beauty of my first poetry book:

Water color art: Ellorien

Cover art: Sandra Fisher Purvine

Photo of me by Cedar Tree: Teri Connolly

Avatar painting of me by Cedar Tree: Jeanette Kahle

Rune photos: Billie Sage

May we all find peace within on our journeys.

Ansuz

Table of Contents

BRANCH 1

Past Remembers

I fight this that I am, because my past I do wish to please. The past remembers me not. Why, then, do I put Billie in this spot? Love seems to escape me, though believe in it, most adamantly I do. Others see worth in this old soul, amazing person, are you. What eyes do they use to see me? When in the mirror I see invisibility, when looking deep inside I see little girl lost. The past now I must leave to be able to live in all I believe. What thorn would hurt less? I ask thee to come to me now.

Being Me

Feeling all like a girl but born in the body of a man, puts me in the social frying pan. The voyeur wants to feel. The doctors want to send a bill. The hater wants to kill. What's all this mean? What's all the ruckus? Put on makeup and create hocus pocus, makes me lose my spiritual focus. All I ever wanted was a little peace inside, so hard to find so I cried. When I am who I am, some of society say I might be the beast. But I'm not evil, or I'm not bad, and all that hate just makes me sad. Someday, me being me will set all that I love free. People will see that Loving the "other" is the way to be. Feeling all like a girl but born in the body of a man, puts me in the social frying pan. Love will change it. Love will win. Love is the only thing that can.

SINGLE TEARDROP

I sit here and wonder what is real, I must have at one time taken the red pill. For days, my head has felt like it is going to pop, the world is mad make it stop. Many a thing I have seen I really left life when I was a teen. It became so much, too much, and I had to decide, how and when I would finish this ride. A simple step I did make, to be real. Is that right or a mistake? Then in my life souls of wisdom began to appear, fill my head with thoughts I never thought I could think. I could be who I am, I made it happen, OMG shazam. I still have many doubts about who I am, what I am about. Then a lesson, a chapter, I did read and wonder if it is true that I could be happy no matter when and no matter who. I will take this into my heart and see if I can truly start, my mind full of turmoil knowing this, that patriarchy needs to stop, for women to live their truths. They have all the universe in a single tear drop.

The Soul is a Rose

Merrily we go where the liquid tide does blow, tear drops turn to snow and Merrily we go, round and round from the top there is oh such a drop, sometimes the wish is for it never to stop, but love catches and wipes the knows. Merrily life is the ride to keep your heart on your toes and so does the fairytale blow, love catches when the mind tells to hell go, round and round Love knows, story blows and the soul is only a rose.

Sunday's Lie

Fallen from forever stars, fighting passion's bars. Long since past the feelings that lust cast. Light says this, and darkness says that, Spirit says wolf and cat. Fallen from forever stars, sticky truths like moldy tars. Heart says Love, but what is really the goddess above? The snake of truth, the crow's law above, guide my soul to turtle dove. When Love I understand and Peace is across my heart's desert sand, forever stars take back the fallen land, this fallen daughter shall rest once more in creations, forever water lore and be healed of the wounds that humanity tore.

Passing By

Passing by I am passing this way. What way you say? White, do I pass? Is race a way to hold others in a slavery class? Gender, for what do I pass? Do you see me as a laddie or a lass? Female or male - what slavery do those words entail? Age, am I old or new? What is old to you? Am I new when I change my clothes? Or are wrinkles the only clue? What slavery do wrinkles set on you? Social - am I rich or poor? Does money make me one of these or does it the ego only please? What slavery has borne and will be because of "social norm"? Passing by - I am passing this way, these and many more will come into play. Passing by passing this way the Love in your heart I say is where we should all start. See the soul Love their infinite part, those others are just ways that slavery starts. Passing by - I am passing this way. Will you let me stay or send me on my way?

Shaman's Life

I died, yes, a certain kind of death, the first time probably different than the rest. Thirteen and nobody to tell me what was happening. All these things - these wrong things- the biology I could not change, did not understand, no one to tell me what I am. The second was the taking, no longer able to stand that awakening, seventeen. Only short years in between, enough to kill three. Still they brought back the breath in me, damn death when will you be with me? Years in between some happy, some sad. Even produce a most amazing little lad. Never awake for me shorting out the wires of history - then the leaving. The third death at forty-nine, alone now. Thought the pain would surely kill, but only brought insanity or perhaps awakening. Still no one to tell me what I am. Only the vision I charge to like a battering ram. I don't remember fear since thirteen yet fear is all that I am, how can that be to be and not be? Perhaps this question is my path to Love, Peace and Spirituality. Three deaths, how many more to go? How many in one lifetime? Now the listening - spirits, guides and teacher - trying to leave my mind behind. Save the mother, weave hearts Love, what madness! Who am I to be such a Reacher? So, tomorrow what is to come? The teacher says still you doubt, the Spider tries to fix and reroute, so tomorrow with fear and without I will see what this may be about. Three deaths all behind, I live, yes, a certain kind, for now we see - if I can handle the Shaman's life.

SATURDAY'S TRUTH

Forlorn and lonely I seek the truth, but being of wavering mind, I can only see that truth for me is blind. My heart, I think, is big, but in chains still it abides, and all that I am fears the mind of hell and where it resides. To passion, I have only fading memory, body flung and flailing, Love in my mind only sailing. What bitter pill would it be if lonely truth is my only reality? Save me not from the unknown, for all my past should I atone, and when man makes his last mistake, then only should the stars I partake and once again be one's daughter, no longer looking upon the ugly slaughter. If you find this sad but true, know that if possible, my heart resides in you.

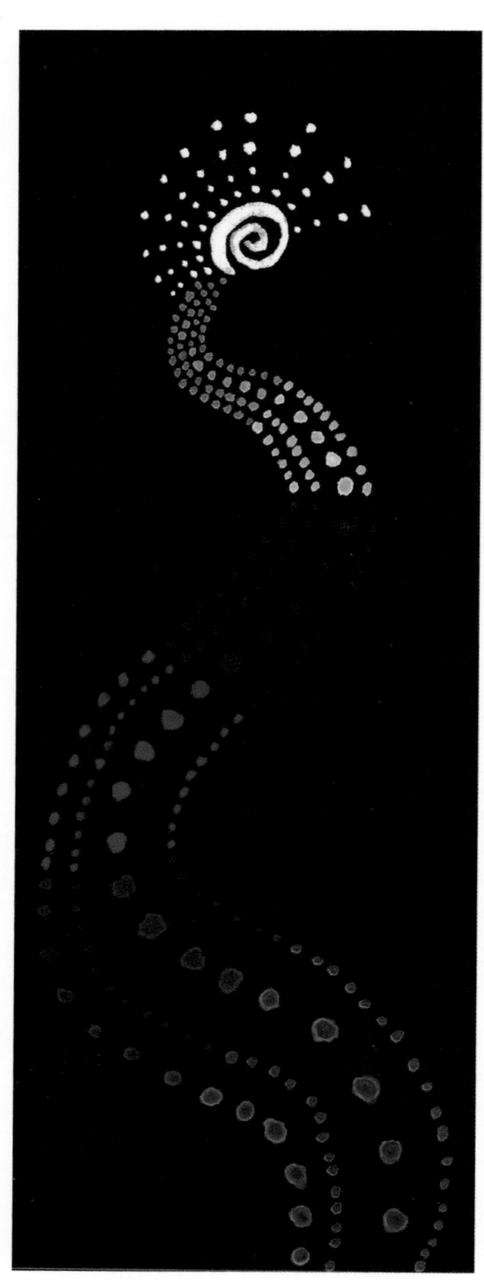

CRICKET'S SONG

Cricket's song in the stillness of the night. Cricket's song, the devil's delight. Cricket's song, a shot rings out. Cricket's song, what has gone wrong? Cricket's song, another is gone, devil's delight. Cricket's song.

Little Girl Blues

Little girl gots the blues. Not the day to look at the news. Gonna love, love the way the universe do. Let the duality leave. Let love believe. Little girl gots the blues. Gonna let her mind play among the trees, let the wind blow her gentle leaves. Little girl gots the blues. Gonna let Love be her news.

That That I am

Why is it I fear that, that I am? Battle, battle, the story rages on, only to end never more. For how can forever end? Question of the soul, folly to the wind. How, pray tell, did such story begin? With blood of the kin, dust that has never been, and Light, hot never-darkness sin. 'Twas started the day before never, blessings been.

Dragons and Butterflies

I have seen in my head dragons and butterflies. Understanding not which is truth and which are lies. The beauty floats and builds snake filled motes. Light above and dark below curling up and seeping in to a man's hard bone. Dragons swoop and butterfly poop, both are real in my eye. There it is high and low unknown which is Love and which not so. Wind blows every day no matter if it is good or evil that play. So, it has always been some come and win and some only sin, but none know if it is the dragon or the butterflies, it is all the same it is only man that gives it the name. So, what is it that makes me care what difference if halo or tail when earth worms and earth are the only smell? Dragons and butterflies, head and eye, it is all just a spot in the one ever lasting lie.

Gender True

I am who I say I am. Really, it's true. Inside is where I am boy or girl, not what appears to you. Since this is true, may I please have dignity, too? If I say my name is Sue, would you please say her and she? That would be so accepting of you. If I say my name is Bob, could you say he and him, even if I am only five foot two? Society says that it's only a lifestyle. This is so untrue. It is simply reality, same as what you feel inside of you. This I know is true: To deny is to suffer; to accept is to be healthier. So, when I accept myself, and dress and act a certain way, it is not to shock you. It is to be healthy in my true gender just like you. Like all, I search for Truth and meaning. So, I ask: Will you welcome me on my journey? As I, in turn, welcome you.

MUSIC

Music, not taste or sight, just the same, the brain and heart at the same time delight. Memories flood from sound's clear tickle. Try and remove the past puts the heart and mind in such a pickle. Some memories so sweet, others dark do meet. What is one to do? Perhaps cry and love today and yesterday too. Music box dancer to my mind an enhancer, hear the sweet notes, and feel the love and the pain. Yesterday, never again. Today, the best ever been.

BRANCH 2

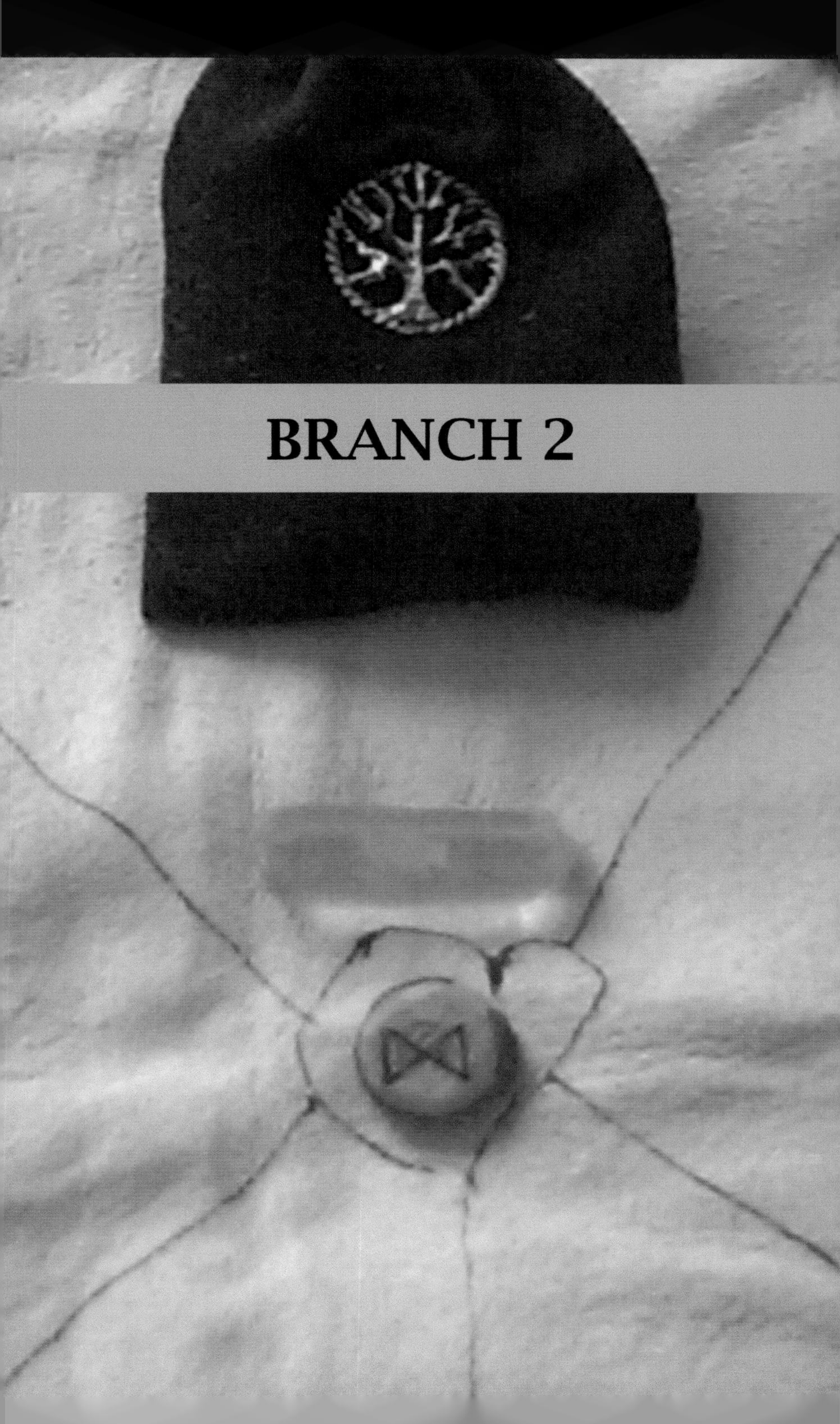

IVORY

Those that say they have the power, hide their lives in high barred ivory towers. Their might, they think, is that they can control you and me. Yet can that be? You, perhaps, live without all their splendor. Weep for their shit and become the pretender. But when awake you do be, see that "things" are only hells to render. Once you step into yourself your heart becomes the Love vendor. You have discovered what they may never recover, the knowing that the one above is the only true lender. So below you now share what is real power, and leave the hiders to wallow, their own shit soon they might swallow. This is not to say you may want the ivory power, but only shall it be yours for one short hour? So, Love is what is and was and will be, so better perhaps to venture within, where once you touch your own soul, through the universe you can stroll.

Sooth

Soothsayer by night, Bard by day, the whole world should listen as I say. But the world turns, there is many a deaf ear, if only they could hear. The age of Love would appear. Truth by night, poem by day, ole Billie is crazy as an upside-down bat is what they say. The old say that Ra was the way, that before science there was only pyramid dust in which to play. Now the new says that there is a force for you mixed up in all life's glue. Soothsayer by night, Bard by day, Love is the glue now and before Ra I say. Look to your right, look to your left, look up look down, looking inside is where the real truth will be found. Truth by night, poem by day, when ole Billie is silent that's when she found Loves way.

FEMININE DAY

As I have backed away from my most feminine day, I wonder if others see I have wandered away. Seems that you must still be XX or XY, or the world says you lie. Male they make me, cause those hormones spent their time in my early days. To those that call me him, never was I a "man," even if that was some small god's plan. Spent time knowing hell. Those days society would have called me "well." Drink towards death. That's okay. It's normal. Be healthy and sane, but not be girl or boy, then you are the devil's toy. Old men who say they know better make insane rules of who you are from the fears that visit them in their closets' pools. Those that were my clan instilled society's backward plan. Still to this day in my head do those trite words and rules show their might. So, wander down a path do I, alone for my fears still I fight. Only sure society for me is not right. Alone, I know, is from me not those on my left or on my right. Worry not, I say. It is not your plight. My most feminine day was yesterday. Today I am what the moment says: silent to hear SHE, that is my heart balance share.

The Way?

There is darkness that is just darkness, there is darkness that is fear. Darkness that is fear sends me demons and daughters, slayers and slaughters, find compassion and calm, stillness and songs. I struggle when I am human and I am human because I do struggle. The light perhaps is the knowing, the knowing that there is vast unknown. Darkness has shot its arrows and sent its pure pleasures, it is the struggle, it is the human treasures, when seen is the Light of Loves, Heart is the measure.

Clock

My heart is rhyming, the clock is timing, things of illusion be subliming. Where is my Love, in my heart or in the great conscience above? Sending glow from within, lighter than snow. How does that compare to the feathers weighted toll? Trolling my mind, heart in The Clutch, spirits soul, can I be such? When I wither on this vain vine Truth will teach me to leave all behind. This darkness is truly Light let your fears leave stage right, as I bid you goodnight.

My Eyes

My eyes, they say, are beautiful. I often wonder what it is they see. Are they open to reality? Do they see what is real? Only I know what my eyes have seen, but only you see what they show, for when I look in them, I only see what my eyes have seen. Was it beauty they saw and therefore what you see? Perhaps one day I will see what it is, this beauty you see. For right now, I only see the lesser me. Love, light my eyes to see, the greater me.

Soul Light

There is no man or woman in my bed, only the Light's love in my heart and my head. On this journey, they say gender is the key. It has been a special journey for me. If gender is the key, then will I ever be free? There is no man or woman in my bed, only the Light's love in my heart and in my head. Love is the way I have heard it often said, but not the love of a man or woman in bed. No, it's the Love glowing from inside, from inside my heart and my head. My heart and soul yearn, but it is the Light's turn. No man or woman in my bed, only the Light's love in my heart and in my head. In this journey, I am being led. To what end? Certainly not another's bed. My eyes cannot see the end; my heart and soul can only grow within. No man or woman in my bed, only the Light's love in my heart and in my head.

Little Billie Sage

Little Billie Sage, she be all the rage, pick up her might and set the world right all the while only being on stage. Shake a rattle, give evil battle, to Boo do tattle. Little Billie Sage, over the top, worked with a mop, and set souls to hop. Little Billie Sage, never the rage, perhaps a mage lives in the little earthen cage. Little Billie Sage, made from Love's page, Peace for heaven's gage.

Transsexual Tears

The flow of life, the flow of tears. Man lives a million years. Will pain ever be in arrears when we reach that million years? Life with love, life with hate. What will be man's fate? Which will be God's tears: Joy that man has learned to heal, or sorrow man has lost his tomorrows? Tears and pain, healing, and joy. Transsexual girl or boy. Tears of sorrow, tears of joy. A million tears. A million years.

Real

I was connected a moment ago. It was real it was in my soul. I dreamed of intelligent spiders and purple crystals that can do amazing things. It was real while I was there. A child of 2 or 3 tells facts of things he couldn't know. He says he doesn't know what he is talking about. It was real. I was there to hear. A little girl says it is a dream, that this is not real. This I was told: that it is real. The things that are real we do deny. When we are told that what see and hear and touch are real. I know that love is the only thing real when all is done. Love is what will carry on. I was connected a moment ago. I felt the stars and hear the moon. I see the galaxy and touch the Love. Love held all of me, not just that which is here. Tell me: What is real?

Silence

The silence is loud and profound at this time when none is around. Come sit in the sun, and live until you are done, then rejoin the One, for we are it, and it is we. I, too, know God is real, for Love is in my soul. All I lack is the knowledge to be whole. When will I understand? When will truth be mine? I think on that day, may perchance, I will float away. Or perhaps I will stay. Who can say? The thing is, I do not know. Nor do I know one who does. For now, it is okay to search, to long and love, but truly I wish to join the sunset above. Love is all that is real. This my soul I hope does heal. For this way, the dark does not steal. The silence is loud, when none are around ....

NEW YEAR

All is new is old again. Let the world spin spin spin, and let Love's work begin. In the end, I am all I was and nothing I am. Look in the mirror. Oh damn, I am the woman I am and never was at all, because of the Love that is and was.

Boxes

When I was born my parents put me in a box. It was not cardboard or wood or metal. It was male. Then I accepted many more boxes over the years, son, sailor, father and failure. I accepted alcoholic and sinner and freak. Then female, transsexual, and searcher. The boxes to me have improved, but boxes are they still, chains and weights, limits and lines. So, I choose now my new name my new box in an effort to be more than whatever box others, or I, start to enclose myself in. My first name is C. It stands to me for my star name, but is not all of it. For I want this not to be my next box but an opening to what is. My middle name is Iam. For I am part of the Source. I am from the yin and the yang, I am from the eternal then, now and always. I believe many of you will say I am this or that for having said this, but those are your boxes to define me, and that is fine, but I will not stay inside of your box or mine. I wish to evolve and understand what Love means and live what it means. My last name is Morethan. It means that whatever box I, or you start to put me in, I will do my very best to be more than that box. All of you are equal to this and more than this. It is only my little way of breaking free from the limits that are unreal and unneeded. And I hope that each who reads this can find their own boxes and fly where we belong. Journey well. Search for what limits you, and Love it, and fly past it. Become the universe! For you are already. Find the peace within, and share it with yourself and all that you imagine.

ABOUT?

Here we come into the world. Spend our life trying to figure out what it's all about. Sing or shout? Shoot or toot? Live like Buddha? Or make lots of loot? In the end, you should've just loved. For all will feel Death's harsh boot...

BRANCH 3

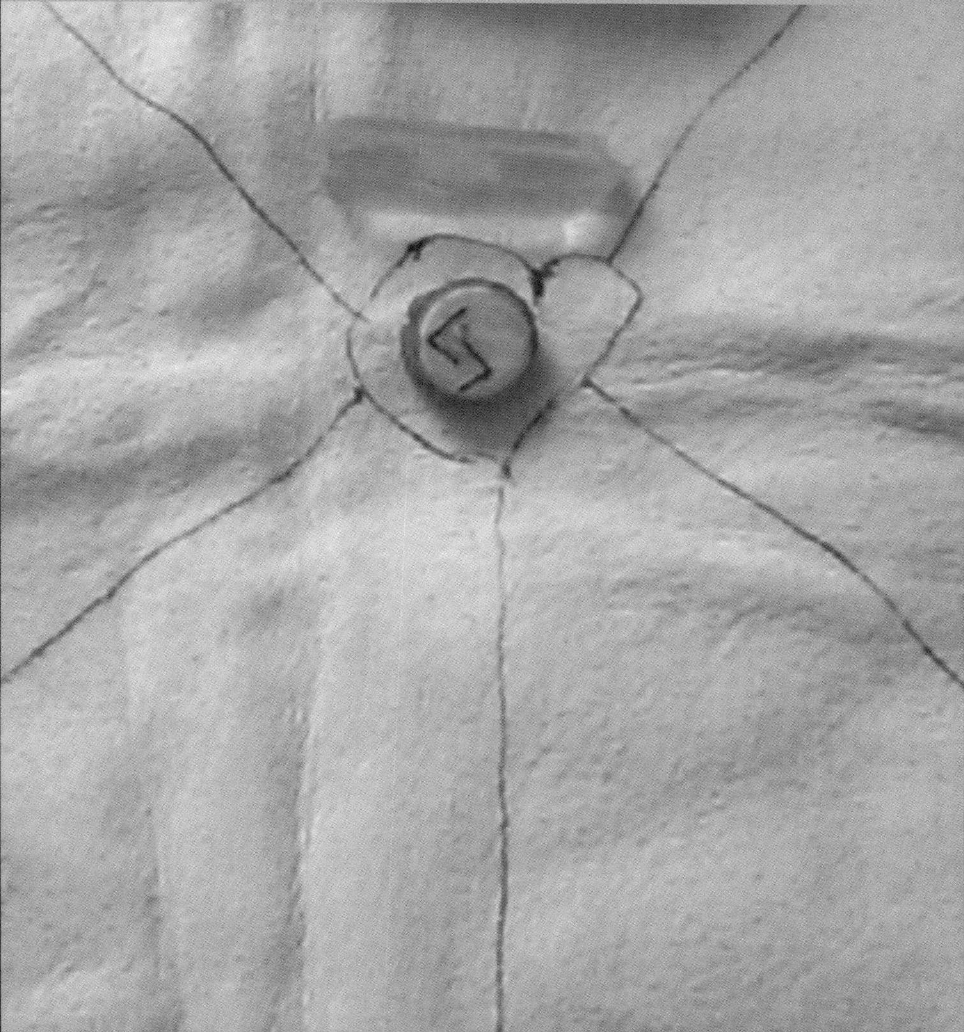

MAGIC GONE?

My heart flies into my soul memories of dragon's fairy's and trolls, where have they gone I asked the Goddess? Well nowhere, they all still live in your eye, all you have to do is leave your brain behind and let your heart touch your soul for there lives your every goal. Then magic began to swirl and I began to twirl as my heart touched my soul I was sailing a giant ship in a fruit bowl. The stars were out waving and singing, wanting to see what I was all about, so I waved back and smiled a crescent moon, and my tooth began to sing an old Irish tune. As I sang the Goddess cried and her tears made a river wide and brought me to her lovely side, we held hands and floated across the galaxies color, they all were so beautiful and smelled of popcorn butter. We sailed and sailed for centuries I'm sure the beauty of it all became a blur. Soon we sat and talked as we walked the beach of eternity, and I wondered how I walked and sat at the same time, but soon forgot because the sea turned to lemon lime. After a while the Goddess said we must return and I asked if I couldn't stay for a little while. She smiled and said you are always here, your magic large and strong, all you have to do is ring the gong and leave your mind behind as your heart floats into your soul. Now I sit and watch the sunset and smile knowing what I know, that the brain is nothing when my heart is in my soul.

Water's Song

I walk up the trail. Dreams still linger in my mind. The tree's green, light against the blue sky. The sun warm, yet not high. As I walk up, the earth beckons me, whispers in my mind "welcome home." The water flows and whispers its song gently to me and to all that would listen. Up ahead the sound of falling water. I come and sit and listen to its song. I sing back and am one. The dream is no longer, the song having taken its place.

3

I never had a love, you see. I had 3. There was you mom, though mother and daughter we could never be. Then I had you, my wife. Never ever did I think I would have a wife. Thought I would die alone, crazy. Me having a wife changed my very life. Then that love brought down our boy from above. Didn't think I could love any more than you, my wife, but man, that boy... That's a love I never ever thought I could feel. Seeing him born, that's when I met Love. My soul I could feel. Well I never was no good at showing anyone what I felt, probably because my mind told me I had the wrong pelt. Well this life maybe I didn't do it the way most understand, but love times 3 is what my heart thinks is grand. I never had a love, you see. I had 3. Then, now, and for infinity. I wrote this little poem cause I felt my soul was alone, but Spirit said, "Looky here! Open your heart, and all your love is always near." I cried, and it felt good. For you see, I never had a love.

To this point I have had at least 3.

THOUGHTS ON CHANGE

How did change begin? Did the God entity stick a finger in the pool of energy and matter starting ripples of change--ever ending expanding out ripples of life and stars and galaxies? Or did the nothingness blow up one day, making such a big bang that waves of change move ever out away from the awful noise of creation? Little matter, I think, as here we are far from the beginning, all of our little ripples expanding out from our beginning, barely touching others or meshing fully in their ripples. This is all good, for to stop the positive change of moving forward is to stagnate or wither and die. Change is life. Change is always. Without change, there is no more.... The most amazing change I have read about is that of a caterpillar living its little life crawling along. Feeling the change of season, it builds itself a cocoon and slowly dissolves itself into a liquid pool of the essence of life and begins reforming itself anew to emerge another day with wings and beautiful colors to live its change to its end in flight and magic.... leading me to believe that nothing is impossible. So, if you think you might be stagnating remember the butterfly and remember its beginning and reshape, change, move forward with creation as it moves its ripples of change ever out positively out to the end--or is it the beginning... for you are a part of it all. Without you, the Universe is incomplete.

LIGHTED RAIN

I stand in lighted rain. God's tears wash away the Pain. I stand in lighted rain. Heart full of Love. I stand in lighted rain. Which will be the way to share? I stand in lighted rain. Feel its touch. I stand in Lighted rain. How will I understand? I stand in lighted rain. Alone. I stand in lighted rain. Awash in awe. I stand in lighted rain. It stopped.

Sight of Glory

The Mother does add her beauty to the heavens, glowing with deadly beauty, eternal lightning starting the heartbeat of the morning, rise and breathe in the morning dew, avert thine eye for it will burn at the sight of glory from below and above. Pray thee for her awakened kiss and burn in her desire.

LOVE IS MAGIC

Love is magic. Magic is wind, water, earth, and air, Heart and love are a pair. In all do they live and create the power of three - the seed of you and of the tree. Live fully your life and bounty be yours - but never strife. Live for love, for you make divine feminine shine. Like starlight off the edge of the sharpest knife.

Know What You Know

There is magic right in front of our eyes, yet science fills us with its surmise. We breathe in fairy dust, yet do not smell it because we love with carnal lust. Our ears miss the whispers of millions of years, for we get lost in brewery's beers. Yet all is not lost for you can change it all with a few cleansing tears. The griffon talons grip the moons silvery glow and darts in and out of thousand-year-old snow. The fairy's hat smells as perfect as nectar clear, when your nose is over there not here. The breeze whispers songs of lives past, forever will they sing and last. How might I see these wondrous things you might ask. Well I am not perfect at it as of yet, but of what I have had I will try let. Stare at the moon as you walk and let its light fill you with flight, sit under a 500-year-old Cedar tree and listen as it begins to talk with ye. Giggle as a flower tickles your nose and leave the shiny to let them know you know why. Listen as you walk in the wind, for it is pure magic where it has been. Then when you feel your heart beat Leave a tear for Mother to let her know you love her sweet. Most of all let your tears flow because all this magic has struck you so, because in your heart of soul, you know what you know.

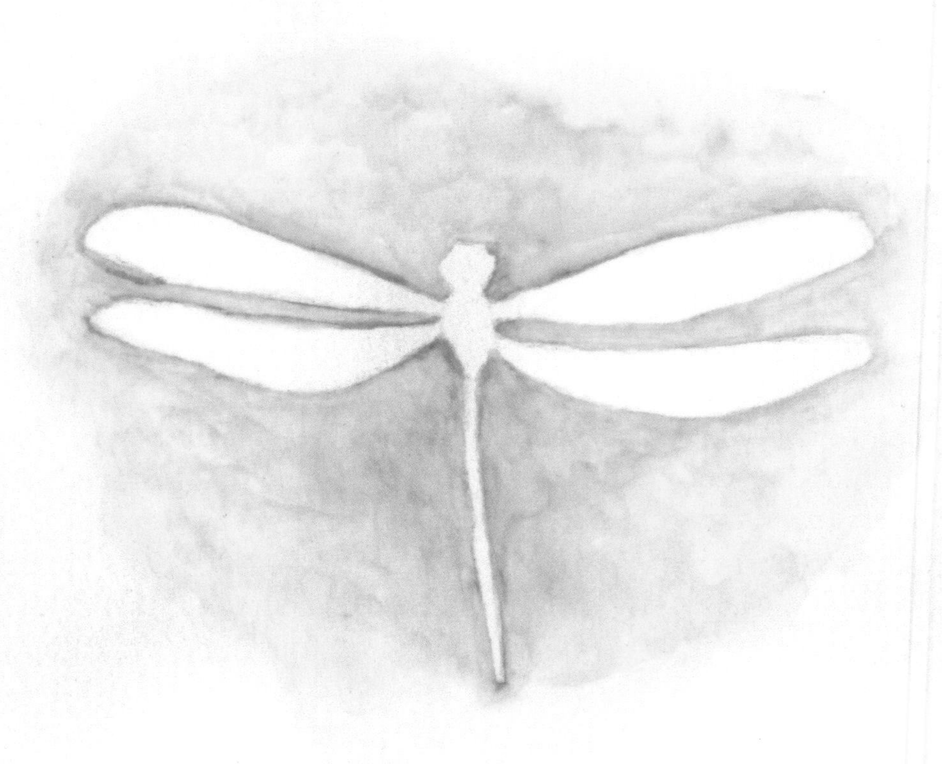

THE STORM

At work a passing thought, I need to cry. No reason I don't know why, there and then my eyes were dry. Time to go flashes way off, put on wind breaker in case it might shower. Two blocks into the seven home, rain starts to hit me with heavenly power. Shoes and pants soaked in a moment, splash in the gutter, laugh and sputter. Two blocks to go take cover for moment so hard to see, still smiles and a heart full of glee. In the house out of wet cloths, go to the porch to sit and see mother's throws. The lighting here now, crack two, my eyes see four, rain begins to pour. Hit so close, light burns sight of eyes, jagged line from heaven to hell, house shakes like a ringing bell. The beauty sends my soul high, not afraid, not to cower, my eyes flow from being alive to see such power. I chant with the rains drumming flow, asking this moment not to go. A passing thought, no longer a need to cry. My soul to yours Loves answers why.

SKIP A ROCK

See the water. See the stone. Skip a rock. Listen to the ripples talk. Walk in grass with no socks. Touch a tree. Learn to see. Breathe the air. Turn off the thought. Talk to Mother while on a walk.

LOVE'S TRUE LOVE

Love's true love is bone and blood from stardust and waves above. Life's breath is a gentle thing, for true love does it bring. But time is a fearful trap, and to dust, blood, and bone it does bring. So, sad we sing and dance and play to pretend to keep the dust away. But the Light does begin to shine and show the lie of linear time. So, when the soul does learn, dust will no longer be that one's turn. The way of Love will be joy's dance and be forever's chance. Chose thee the Light, and learn of stardust's true Love.

Desert Wind

Desert wind blows to try to dry me, yet she cools and revives me. Desert wind wiggles the leaves and waves to me, blows the clouds to form imaginings of my mind. Desert wind whispers and brings a tear to the corner of my eye, even as she blows it dry. The wind whispers and tells no lies, as she blows to send my heart to love in the sky.

MIST

What I say or write matters, or it does not matter at all? And it does this all at the same time or not at all. Infinite possibility, never-ending time, are all really just sublime, when within the spark of Love is Light or dark. Only the moment matters, and it does not exist, so just one, one more musing in the mist.

The Howl

Walking home at 1:30am. Clouds move slowly across a near-full moon that peeks in and out of them. The warm temps have water in the alley with old, dead, musty leaves. The smell is pungent. Some of the dry one's rustle on the cold cement. I look up at the clouds and moon, and I had to, yes, I had to howl, like the long-removed cousin, the wolf, crying at my love of the moment and the mystery.

BRANCH 4

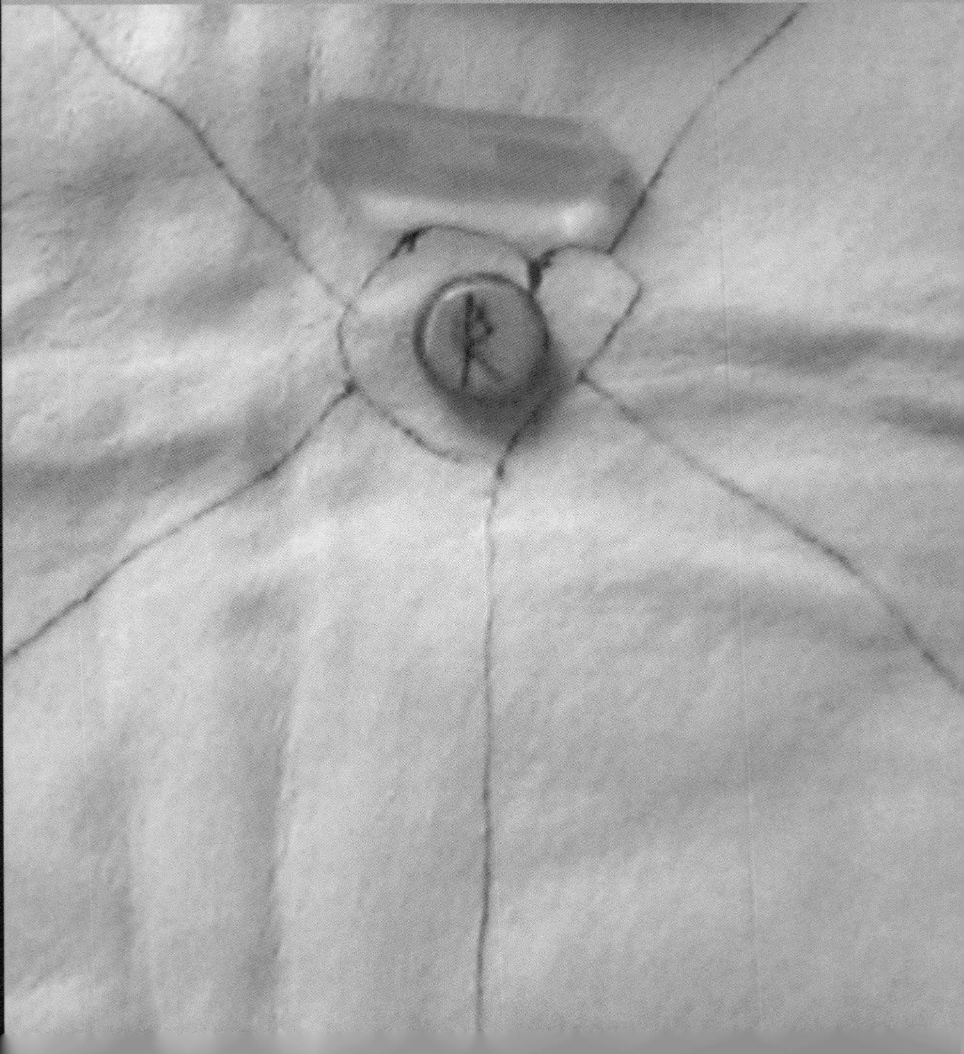

Love's Wait

Love now has always been, or is now time to begin? Love to be shall come to be when Love's true heart becomes you and me. It has always been and is yet to be, Love's true way is you today. Tomorrow is not too late, for Love has always been the Light's true weight. See your heart is now to Love, for you have always been from above. To begin, you must love, for that has always been. You are Love's true form before even you are ever born. Love is what you must do, and all know deeply that is what is true. So now, not wait. For today is tomorrow, and Love is never late.

Wolf and Wind

Wolf and wind with me always they have been. Whispers and cry, Love and lies they have always been. Carried up to the stars on wolf's howl, rustle the leaves under moonlights breeze, two has always been. When two are one, wolves and wind, never will have always been. Wolf's cry seen with my single eye, winds whisper to ear and sky.

The Traveler

I am, the traveler going from alpha to omega, learning that knowing is not and wisdom is only in that one tiny little spot, that what is, is not, and what could be is sunk in some fertile plot. There is pain and sorrow or there is not, there is love and peace and there is not. All the sands of time fit on the surface of a colossal dime, that seven by seven by seven thousand words would only make a one word rhyme. This the traveler has gotten from worlds sweet and rotten. Witnessed nothing and then let it be forgotten, touched the hand of truth and lost it in empty fullness under Orion's roof. All of this is only proof that all does and doesn't matter and Love is the only ascension ladder. I am, the traveler one tiny soul that Loves that you all matter.

TIME'S EYE

Mind-song slithering along Love's line, only a blink in time's eye. When time comes, it goes, and oddly lovely star toes. When shadow falls, winter's heat, when all Spirit's Love does meet. To this, make no sense for your mind-song is only from where you are heaven sent. The heart is more the power. The mind-song only longs this hour. So, when it is time to leave, that is when we will meet.

BILLIE'S PRAYER

My darkness is mine to shed light on and to choose the good rather than the bad. The darkness of the world is all of ours to shed light on and choose the good rather than the bad. Shine your Light, and let Love be what you want the world to be. So much truth is hidden from us. Why? I do not know exactly, but I know that I can change my truth. I, today, this moment, change my truth to not excepting hidden truth. I will look inside myself for answers and believe that truth will start to be revealed. As always, I choose Love this second. This is how I and all of you can change what is. I no longer accept that I need to pay to live on a planet I was born on. The illusions of money and power over me will start to change this moment. I do not accept a one world government that has a few enslaving the many for their own greed. I do accept a one world community where all are responsible, Loving, and caring for their World, not just their own country or village. This is what I can do. I cannot save the world, but I can Love it and become the most Loving evolved being on it that I am able.

Dancing Fairies

The gods are light - the gods are dark - only dancing fairies can ignite - the Love spark. They dance - all as on the head of a pin - hardly do they notice - Love's wonder. Only your heart do they come to plunder. When the gods tell you, you are from the sky - laugh and dance. For it is the fairies that make you fly.

Badass Hippie

My soul in this solid land, only without ETHER in my hand. Soon to come my open, heart LIGHT badass hippie smites with LOVE unite. Then the world will spin and all will show where they have been. And KNOW the ONES might when ETHER lives three days as night. And brings back MAGIC as their souls measure lite. Fear not for this is only prose not the ramblings falling out of TITANS nose. Print it on the leaf like those of old and send it out were the WIND is told. This is true or not only you can tell if you should burn hot.

FALL WINDS

Fall winds silently blew me home, the quiet dark night enveloping me as I pass this light and that, feeling alone, so alone in a city asleep that cares not that one small girl passes through it, riding the winds when they are not watching.

A Cur Lad

A cur lad and I, we travel the night in slither and flight. Our undead days lead to frightful night. The light promises to break our bonds, reflecting into the corners of unseemly dust. Breaking our bonds and standing by love is the must. It is only this... this love that give I trust.

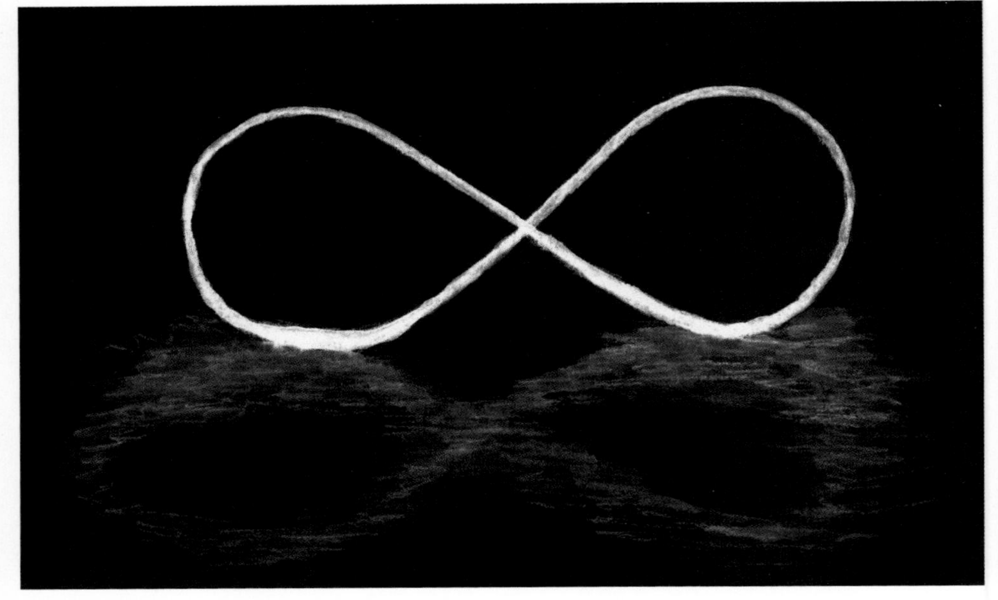

Point of No Return

Once in the darkness the soul did roam, never and now was where it was lost at home. In the vast closeness that is infinity, a tiny light, a spark perhaps of divinity. Un-fear and a step toward the Light. The weight untold, perhaps the child was born of something very old. The quest and the heart, where was one so young to start? Could the millionth step be where it began? Let the soul into that harsh soft land so the journey and the Love came from below, which is above, and as the Light of Love began to burn the soul realized it had found...the point of no return.

Shimmer

Tree leaves shimmer in sunset's glimmer. The dusk of this day is now here. Walk to tomorrow. That is the plan. Hearts from the past all across the land. Strength needed, sad that the light goes, but Love is always there and forever grows.

My Ego

It’s my ego, lets me cry. It’s my soul, lets me fly. I can only choose that is all I have, oh being human what a spot. Now that I know nothing at all, when was it that Boo was going to call? When is time not going to be? Soon or when I am a Red Wood Tree? It doesn't really matter for I am now and then, only using keys instead of a pen. I rattle on and twirl the limb, there really is no difference between me and a sim. So, I will go throw my weekly rock and let all that is master and mock. It’s okay it’s my ego, let’s me cry. It’s my soul that knows how to fly.

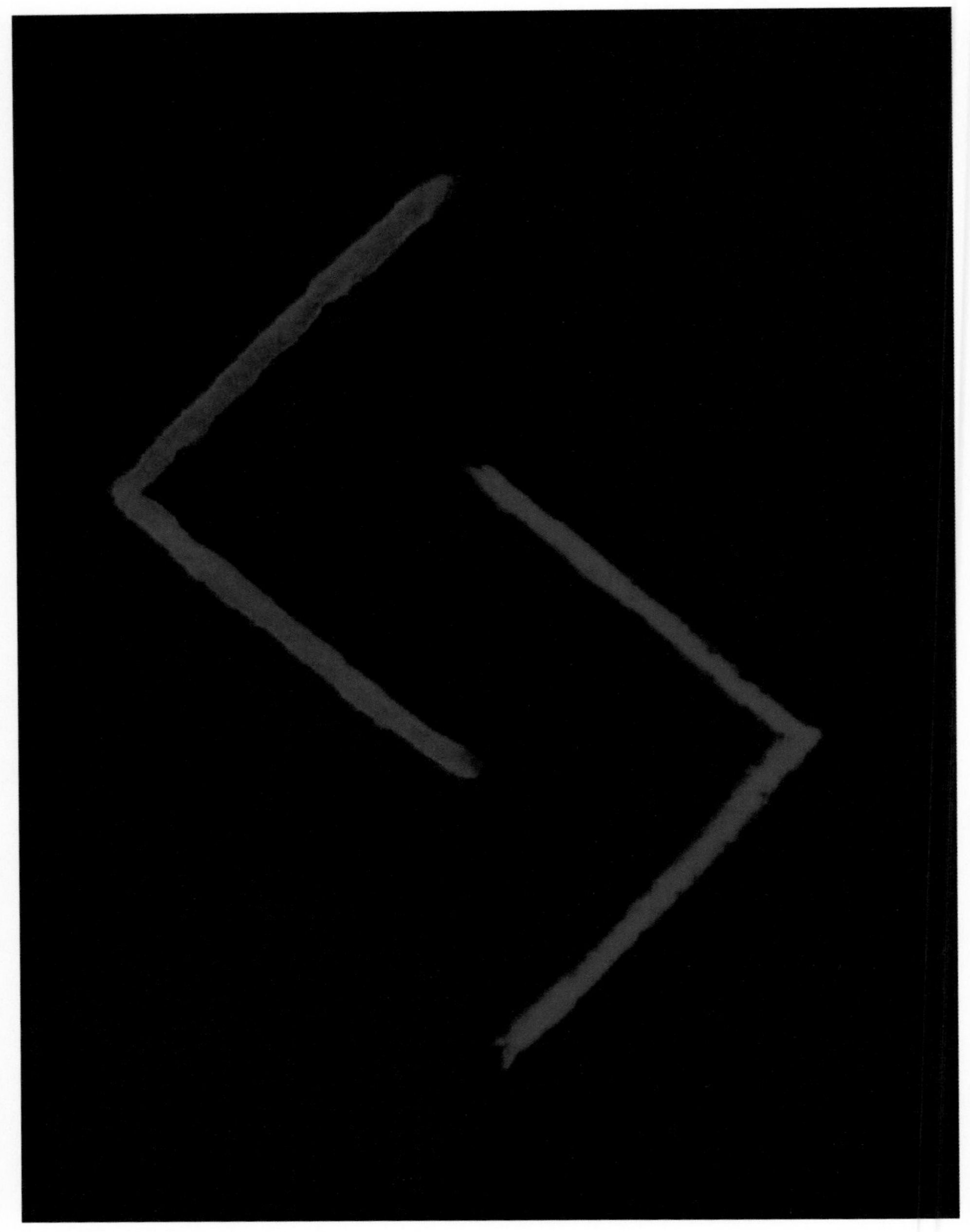

PASSION'S JOURNEY

The water has passion. It flows to its destiny. The earth has passion and spins to eternity. The stars have passion and light the journey. She pretends that the pain in her heart is infirmity and stands stoic for Loves eternity. Silent hours burn her while she dreams of what could have been her passion's journey. Half a soul is her weight, Love split asunder. Only Love's stars await to plunder. To wait her time, the other half do I opine. The Light will not extinguish, for Love's half weight. Were not her deeds untold? What Goddess would be thee, other half my mold? Someday when Love grows old, half her soul will return, if in life if she was bold. While she waits this celestial plot to unfold, I pray my half soul does not die in the cold. The tears she sheds, grow Love’s heart flower, for in this human form, it is her only power. For when those tears do fall, it is her cry to eternity. Call and then the half finds the other. Her pain will end in passion's journey.

DAY'S POEM

The sun is here. The days go by. Sometimes, I wish I could fly. I would go to the clouds and be with God and know all is right, but now, here comes the night, filled with fear and fright. Hold me tight, and help me make it through another night.

BRANCH 5

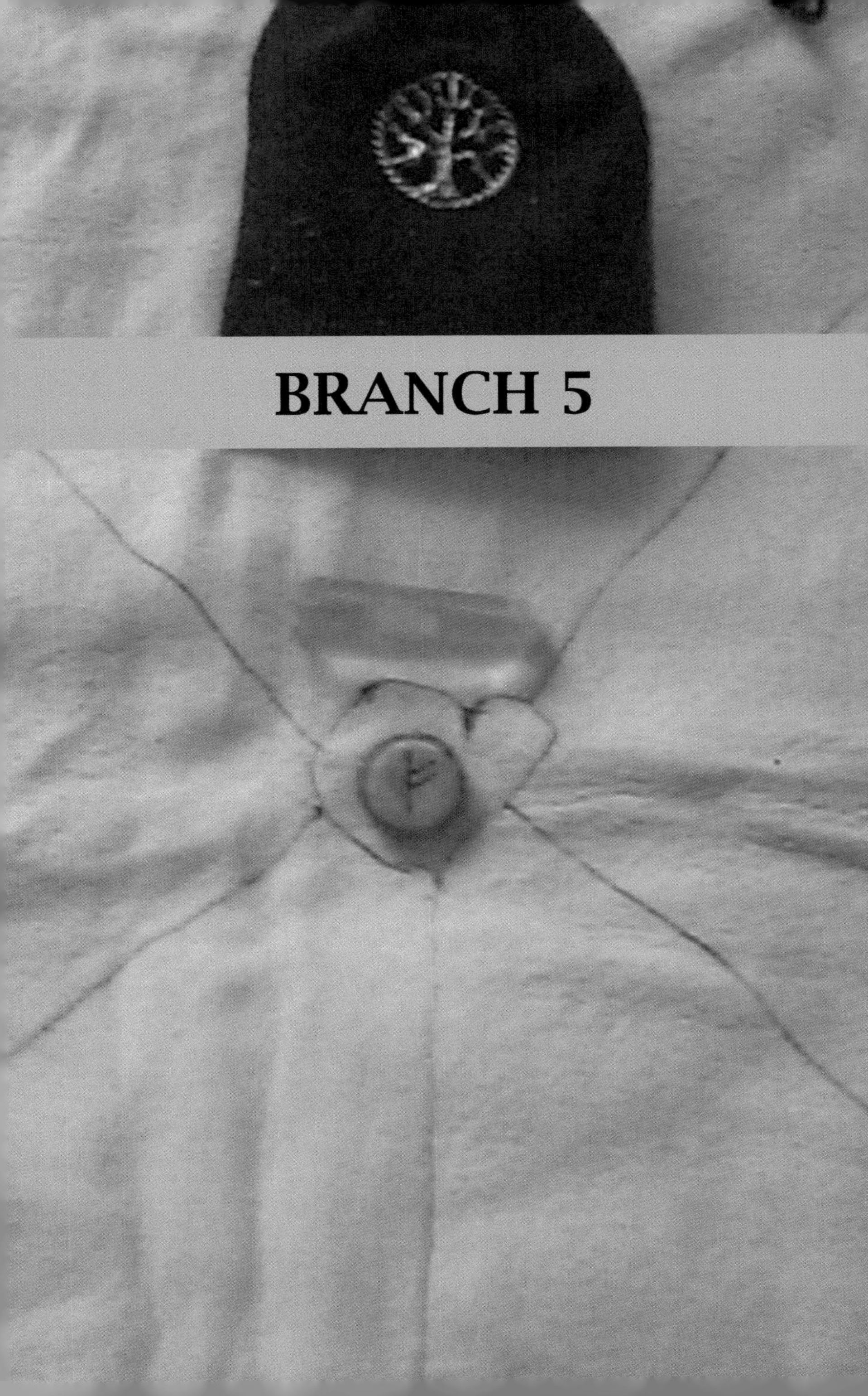

WOVEN

The tapestry unfolds. Little threads create the picture each one of us woven into all, lost. And yet if pulled out, something would unravel. You are the fabric of God in and out of all eternity. You are not threadbare, even if you be from beginning to end.

Heaven's Hell

What do you call hell? I know mine very well. Been down some roads that no one did I tell. Maybe you been there too. Sure, I say some of the surface stuff, but compared to darkness I have known, it's probably mostly fluff. Mine or yours, it is all pretty rough, when we let ego take care of our stuff. The soul grows tired and says that's enough! But what is heaven's hell that makes me tough? So, if you ask, I might say, but most likely I will just walk away, and try to stay on Love's narrow highway.

THE DARKNESS

Tonight, I am afraid of the darkness. Not the darkness of a moonless night or deep in a cave at night. Oh no, those are outside of me, the darkness I fear tonight grips my heart, and squeezes it until I cry like the frightened child that has lost its security. This darkness sends little swirling fingers from my heart to my mind and teases the fear out of every corner I have chased it to. It laughs at the ease it has in flowing through the electrical field of my toes up to my groin, twisting little knots into the yards of intestines squirming to find a little dot of light. Up through my choking throat into the backs of my red lined eyes. Where did this darkness come from? It comes from the story, the dance, the song, the hope that there is meaning. The dragon she is always there, waiting, wanting, knowing what I cannot. So, I sit in my brightly lit room typing on a little machine, letting the dragon know I have fought her before and made her my friend. And I will do so again, one more time, for whenever I ask, "is it time to go home?", the answer is not yet. Soon my light will send the darkness back to the corners and I will be able to lay down my head and sleep once more. I know you will all understand this for I am told you are only me. So, dance your dance and I will dance mine and somewhere, somewhen our souls will recombine and no longer will we have time.

FLICKERING CANDLE

Flickering candle light is near my soul, inside out people see what wavering is in the heart of me. The day did tally what story's belief transitory is thine grief. For folly is what should not be, but listening to ciss is a bane to me. I know this is scales to tip and only mine own heart do I rip. Flicker is the light I see with in me, when listening to proven blasphemy. So, in I go to see what will mend my hearts glow, when feathers weight is only my bait in tow. On the morrow, new light will shine for Boo is a friend of mine, Love wavers and flickers like candle light when fear is what is only story's fancy flight.

I Wonder Upon a Star

I wonder upon a star, I really wonder what is far. When Willow Wisps sing and bells forget how to ring. When time is done even though it really never understood the sun. Time to go - heaven is above and I am below. West is where the sun will rise. When the lie of truth be told, mother's milk will turn cold. Time will turn a backward hand, but have no unrest. Love of Love is only the best. Buddha mentioned there is no time, that is why you must read the poets rhyme. So, sit and stare at these words and I will wonder upon a star.

MOTHER

She now is no longer in our care. She has left and gone to the everywhere. Every when she does now see and gives true love to all. That is as it should be. For long she did not know, now she sees and knows you are strong. Be she here or there, be love in your heart, knowing now we are in her care. My memories will endure, of this I am sure. Blue velvet will now touch my soul. And mother will be in her chair. Be in our heart forever more. Mother farewell...

SILENT ECHO

Ahh silent echo is what I can hear in the empty beating of my heart, for it is lost in eternity sent there from maternity. If ever it knew the truth of Love it was lost in the noise of all truth which was lost to me in my blossoming youth. Look with thine eyes some mystics cried, so I tried, silent visions. Hear with thine ears some masters cheered, so I tried, silent echoes. Understand from thine heart poets spoke, so I tried, silent words. Then to show me the truth of all, the One said you must know it so very small, so I searched, silent knowledge. When I knew that I knew my hearts beat, that Love was life, all I could hear was the silent echo of what was not, for the One had never forgot.

THE JOURNEY

From the depths of hate I arose, my heart sad from years of pain. All that was left were thoughts of death. The hate was for me, the never-ending cry that the freak was I. My end being near, I approached the Light in a tear. The Love arose again and smothered the pain within. Would I this time believe? That Love would the hate and pain relieve? Slowly the crawl to life. The change without slow and steady. The change within leaps when Love said, my heart be ready. My mind, now hungry, forages for knowledge. My heart willing to give the Love. I, yet knowing that more is needed to be ready. The prophets say Love. I need to agree. The world ready for change, evolution about to take another quantum bound. The Love must be without thought of return. Will acceptance be mine? The others am I, but no longer do I cry, for the Love takes death away. Soon my change will be near complete. To accept I must die one more time. Will it be enough? Time will tell whether Billie can be well, or continue to reside in hell.

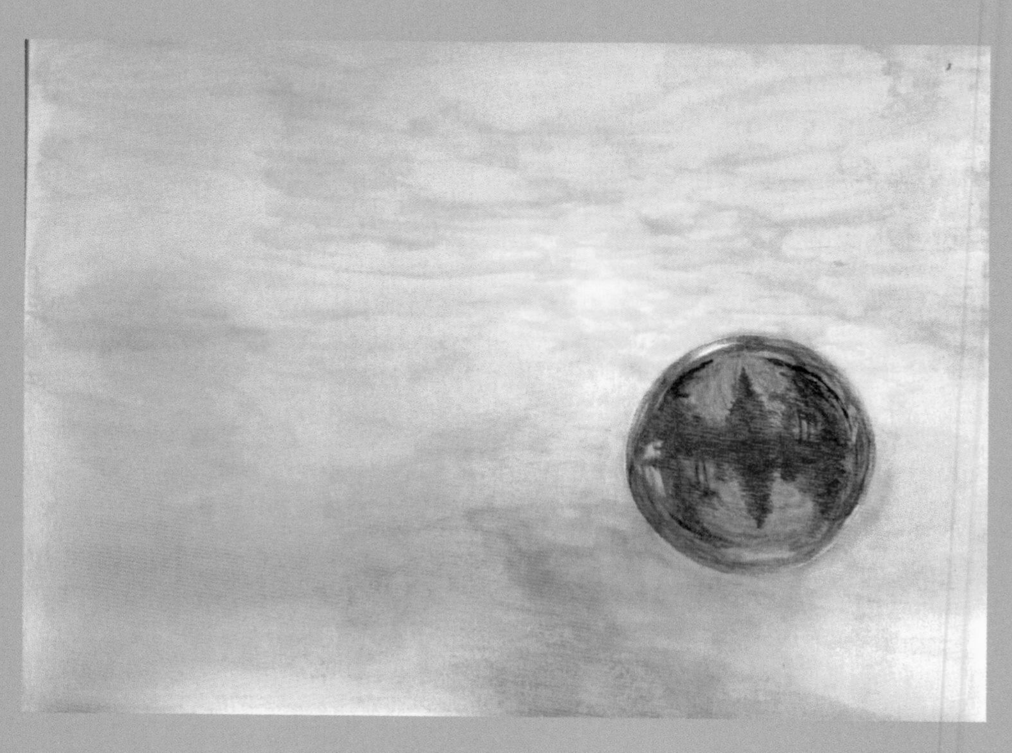

The Fighter Inside

The fighter within has gotten me here. From the time where the fighter was outside, and I pushed it in, how long ago has that been? The fighter raged on an innocent soul and sent the young I to excrements hole. That fighter somehow kept inside sent help to me when darker I wanted booze and pills to be my demise. How is this so? And why? When of life I did not cry. The outer shell finding ways to create my perfect hell. The fighter inside sending me over many years a path that one day may make me well. Healers in my path say I must thank that fighter inside me to help me grow. To do this I have been slow. For how does one thank the years of non- flowing tears? How to praise what made life hell's maze? Even the word itself is not what the present I idolize. But now, the truth be told, I sit and think of things bold. The hell I imagined since when I was not very old is fading as I learn to sit in Love's mold. The world yet old is given Love's hold. I grow from within where that fighter has always been. The past you I did blast hating that I was made to last, but now I am starting to understand: What's past is past, and now I must I must thank you for helping me last. Last from the past and become Love. Thank you, dear me whom I despise, for opening my long-shut eyes. Thank you, fine fighter inside, for letting me exist and no longer hide.

House of Pain

Hate is where I did arise. The world and men did I despise, for all my reality did seem to be lies. The body was the wrong house. I was a dog and not a mouse. The time was moving showing such pain that only brown liquid is what I fed my brain. I tried to show one some trust, and he gave me in return only painful thrusts. Hate of the world and of men is what I became again. Many years my soul did hide. It hated this painful ride. When I could manage I did peek outside. Wondered if death of house was the true ride. The months became years and still inside, my hate still did reside. The house I did change. All my furnishings did I rearrange. The pain did stay blue. It kept the old with some new. The mouse did appear, the dog, though, still here. Mouse did love, so she did claim, but the soul still did hate and blame. Then reality became a swirl, and the mind set a whirl. Love's a jest. Pain is where life rests. This seemed true but was the illusion. She set out on quest to undo the confusion. Sacred is all, and forgive all others, the snake lives only in you, not others. The heart and mind now are near the same, knowing now the mouse must forgive itself the blame. No matter the house or how it began its pain, love its own foundation is a truer game. Any master says it the same: Love is what is and must be the final name.

Passion's Boon

Yes. I know well about my self-esteem - how missing, how fragile, for most of my life's while. No, this moment I will ignore that I might harm that littleness of self, and say how sad my body was born this way. Maybe it is why passion I have always left to others - for what is passion when ego is forlorn. I know I have my health and so many a thing. I know how little my heart to beat this way. But when Love's greatest gift has slithered past the falling years. I cannot help but cry these tiny bitter tears. I know I have missed and pushed away and laughed rather than let in passion's way. For always in my tiny mind is ego's wish of a shapely behind. So perhaps I envy most those that were born with the mother's host, and when I am not in my most sane mind, I anger at the one's humor unkind. Yes, I know well my self-esteem, and favor not this human team. For when my heart does cry, I only see the salty tears of this gender queer eye. No, I cannot leave this lonely place where Love is still my saving grace. Perhaps one day soon the stars and moon will honor my time, in this space with passions boon.

Days of Old

I long for the days of old, when fairies were gay and elves were bold. I long to be the bard that I am telling stories of wonder and burning cold. Magic then filled the air and love and hate were laid bare, songs were sung and holly flung. The night was electric with what was and bee's and sprites were a buzz. The innocence of the maiden's fair and bold worriers were everywhere. What was is still here but only for the weird to hear, so I sit and listen my heart a glisten, the stories rise and I am what my soul does contrive. Soon the time will come or maybe it is here, when weird will be cheered and wisdom will rise from the stone and never again will man make another soul feel alone. For the days of old are never far away or cold for the weird that Love and are bold.

ORACLE

On the 23 of the September, when day equals night and the moon is its biggest bright, all the lords of all heavens will turn the earth to blight. Men will weep when appendages do fall away. For it will be the beginning of Sacred Woman's day. The mighty will turn to dust, and man's biggest structures will begin to rust. For the Meek shall now no longer turn the other cheek. Darkness will swallow Light, and Love will turn round right and those that scoff at Billie will lose their middle member's height. Little kittens will bay at the moon when blood turns the bays maroon, that flows from those who would not dance to the right tune. Inside shall become out, and the others will become the ones with might and slay all those who once laughed at their plight. Tears will fill the rivers full, and all will rue the day of 23. So, says she-no-longer-he: The words are now stone, and men will crumble like broken bone.

--Inspired by David M.

DARK CANOPY

Dark canopy covers my weary soul. Dark canopy to shade the hole where past's love lingers no longer. Dark canopy, Light's Love adores thee. Dark canopy, soul's cloud for fairer days. Dark canopy, my hole beckons thee.

BRANCH 6

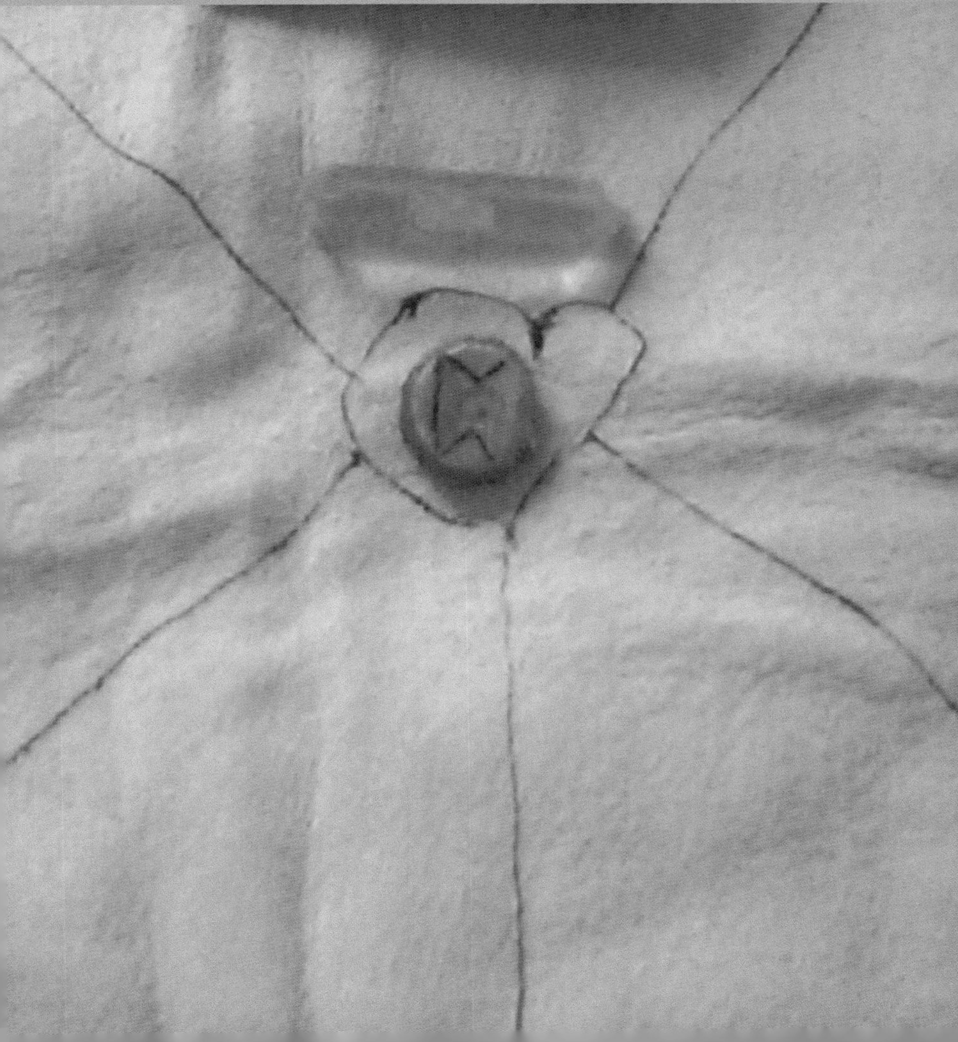

My Thoughts of God

The Light was without. The Light was kept out. The Light was sought out. The Light was the way out. The Light was no longer kept out. The Light was the way out. The Light let her out. One Light began to shine out. Through her, the Light could work. Accepting of the Light, she ventured out. The road is of the Light. Contact with the Light is the way. No longer the darkness, I pray. With the Light, I pray to stay until my dying day.

Magic Center

Where is magic? Where can it be? Perhaps it resides in the heart of I and thee. It is always near for the listener to hear, for magic opens the humbles ear. The one that can see will see magic in the roots of a tree and bless the Goddess for the blessing of me. Where is the magic, whence does it fly? Why, of course, it is where the snows lie and never the dragon does cry. Magic is where it has always been, between hell and a grin. Or, when Love whispers in the wind. Where is magic? Where does it hide? It hides in a moonbeam for you to ride if your heart is open so very wide. Never will you see the magic or hear its tune if LOVE is not your special rune. So, ask not where magic is of me, for it is in the very center of thee.

SLEEP

From my toes to my nose, from a rock to a rose, my eyes now do close. Sleep may come and soon will go. The stars are my true home. There one day I will roam, but for now, sand and bone and sing Love's tone.

Star Sand

What is my path? Where is my way? Am I immortal or here for just a day? When I ask if I can go home, what does that mean? My soul is unseen, and I am seen. Then do we ever merge in-between? Choose my way, or is destiny at play? Why so many questions when I should be in the star sand and play. I am the dreamer, and you are the dream. Come join me in the sandbox and play and laugh at what a thought means.

Love's Star Fire

From the moon's half-light, Love takes my soul in flight. In and out of stars I dodge, gathering the Love's fire. Into my scared ring it does go, and hides there until I point and fire, into your soul, and at that moment, Love will become your highest goal. So, true to you, should you aspire, until you feel Love's star fire.

Clock Crows

From near and far magic is and as a star, what then does reality mar? When fade the illusions son, the dealer is the devil's only one. So, come thee till the clock crows sun, the playground of Alpha is out to shine, where Omega is always far behind. What madness does truth believe when magic wavers and tickles pinecones seed? All is meaning till one looks and kisses angels from greater books. So mighty the ether glows flowing up and kissing toes and magic is what only insanity knows. Fear not for near and far magic may be only a twinkling of a star.

GENEROUS

The beautiful sunset, I did ask, "Beauty you are, might I ask you from afar, what Love does my heart bar? When you're gone, may I wish my soul upon a star?" Perhaps that which is will help me remove said bar that Love my flesh may behold. For the universe is generous I am told.

BILLIE'S CRONE

Never the Maiden or the Mother. Only the Crone for these my bones. Love the Universe, I do try. Love for my skin my soul will I never win. For the Crone, books, words, and nature, but know not pleasures of the skin. Less than woman more than man. One of the Universe's children I am. Sleep in stars. Awake in sand. Love will always give me its hand. Follow my path and be Love's Crone. For in life all death must I atone. Never the Maiden or the Mother. To most only ... the Other.

Soul Travels

When I meditate I slowly descend to fire and ice, where the balance is so nice. When I am comfortable there, I slip down to light and dark, where infinity of one is the other pair, and loving balance I inherit between infinite everywhere. While the body is in the chair, in this space the soul travels to always there. Even deeper I can go and enter into vibrations flow, if I make it here, my third eye begins to see Loves beautiful glow, and my soul starts to understand what is above is also what is below. What I see and what I feel is much the same as a seed and a Stars happy squeal as they meet to become what on earth is real. This I share for when you see me and I have a blank stare, perhaps again I have slipped for a moment into Love's forever nowhere.

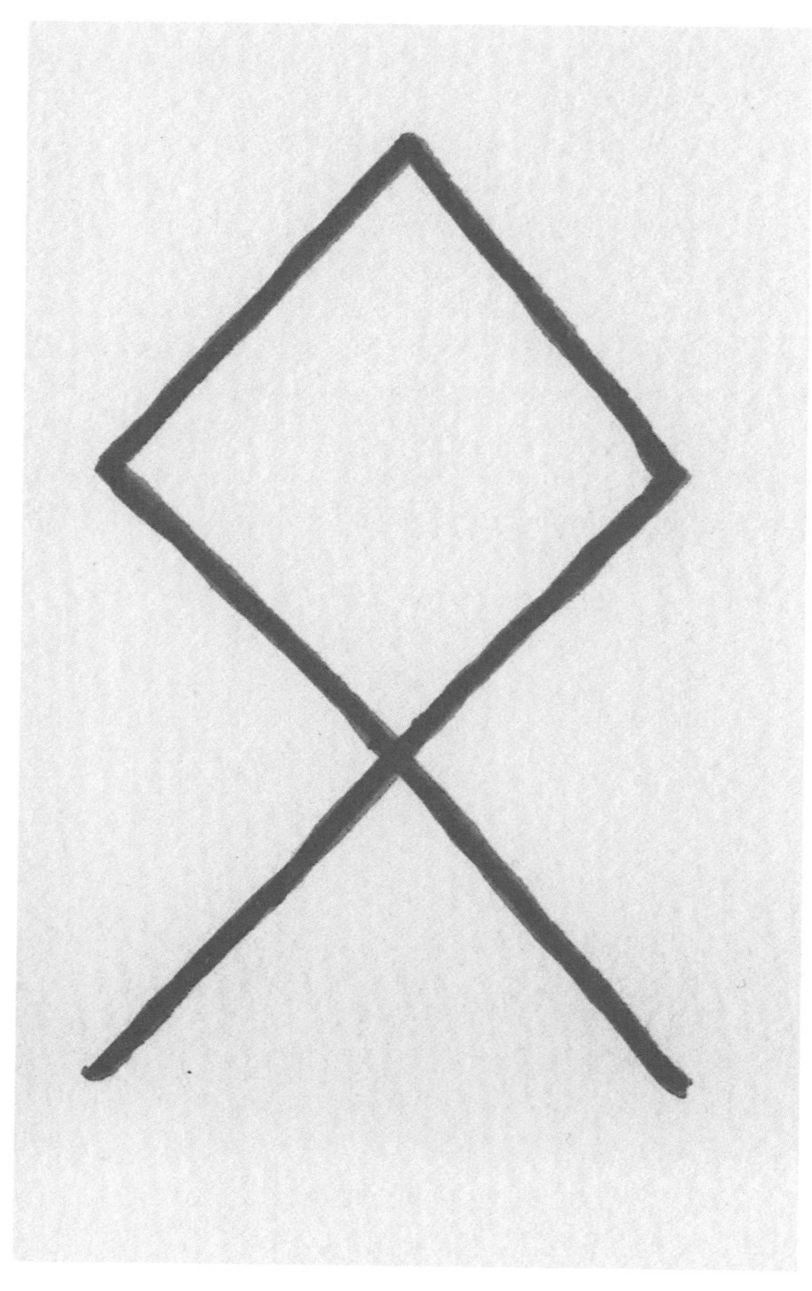

I Am the Star

I saw a star, and in the star, I saw an eye, and in the eye, was a glimmer, and the glimmer was I. and in the I, was a twinkle, and the twinkle was a thought, and the thought was love, and love was I. And the star and I were love and a twinkle.

Little Black Pot

What is, perhaps is not. But what is not? It could be a whole lot. If there is a whole lot of not, would it fit into a little black pot? If not? So what?

SHAMAN SANDS

Sand grains, sacred things, different planes. Feathers and ribbons and mighty birds. Places where time is not there only spirit and love and care. Journey to and fro, make whole the fifteen. As Shamans, they may enter the doors between. SHE that is rode - the waves and wind blessing. The journeys of the new, grains of sand are pearls in the hearts of us that walk in two lands.

DANCE OUR DANCES

I am here to live my drama. Oh, the woes and worries, and then I spy from my all-seeing eye how much Love has gone by. Perhaps I am here for your drama, too. So, if I am, all my heart's love I give to you. Live your drama well, and I will laugh at mine. Dance our dances. Live deeply all our romances. Life's a dream. So, question your questions, and choose all your chances.

LISTEN

Listen... the wind whispers your name gently calling to wake you. Listen.... Love lights you from all around you each connected as you are one. Listen... the wind whispers your name for you are light and the wind. Sleep well dear souls and awaken with your eyes ready to see the play.

BRANCH 7

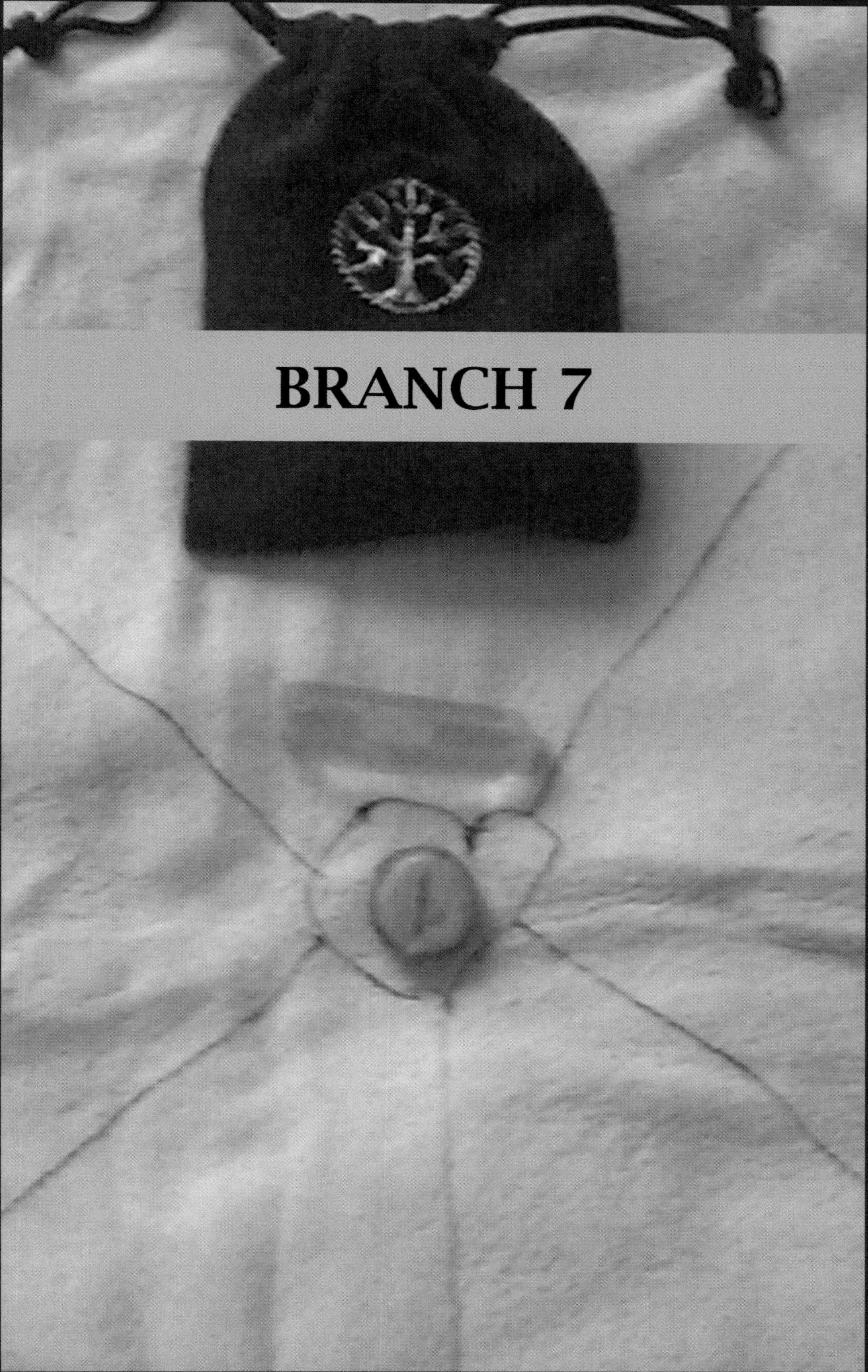

The Old Ones

The old ones they did tell, only now we think it only tale, they did see what we do not and this puts us in a lonely spot. They knew not of heaven or hell, only the above and below and middle shell, the Either they knew would return and glisten until frozen burn. What was then will never be, only what will the tree's sing to me. Hardly a hare does care busy in the minds underwear, listen to what is not true, the past, the future the clear frozen blue. Mount your steads bugle your call, what is, is not at all.

PRELUDE TO PLAIN SIGHT

I am not a seer, prophet, psychic or saint. I was visiting with the seer of Delphi the other day, and I said I had written a poem, but it came to me: only one person would hear it. She said, "Put it on a leaf, and see were the wind does blow it." I was musing this walking away when Moses walked by, so, I asked what he had to say. He said, "Write it in stone, in a most holy tone." So, my mind in the clouds, away I did go when who do I see other than Edgar Cayce. Well, I had heard that he had seen a thing or two, so, I took a chance and asked what he would do. He got a glazed look in his eye and said, "This is for the future to know. However, you have a hangnail on your little toe." With a sigh I limped away, no longer knowing what to do, and I noticed Joan of Arc hitting two rocks together. And I said, "Joan, be careful of sparks!" She was grateful, so this to me she did say, "Billie, be not afraid to be wrong." So here is my little poem you have to hear, since you're here and not home.

Plain Sight

What do I search for? I have been a baby, a child, adolescent, and adult. I have been sober and drunk, dead and alive. What do I search for? I have been a man and a woman and neither and both. I have been pure and evil and sin and delight. What do I search for? I have hated and loved, cried and laughed. I have been fantasy and reality, sinner and saint. What do I search for? I have been full and empty, darkness and light. I have been hunter and fisher, weakness and might. What do I search for? Peace and serenity, the way and the path. I search for me every day and night, when all along I am right this moment A SOUL IN PLAIN SIGHT.

Forgotten Memory

The point betwixt light and dark is so infinite. It seems to not be there at all. One misstep and I am where the other I am used to be. Please love me, hug me, as I will hug thee. The bind-rune is now three, you shall see as if me or all will be as if a forgotten memory.

IN-BETWEEN CHILD

I live in this world not knowing what is real. In a body not boy or girl. Sunsets' rays play over my mind, looking forward remembering what was behind. The days long gone or just begun, will this in-between child know love or fun? What is real? Light or dark? Will this in-between child ever leave a mark? Knowing not truth--the clouds are in the sky, or really do they live in my mind's eye? Many is the time the in-between child just asks… Why?

FEMININE DIVINE

There is the mighty Feminine Divine, keeping all the universe in line. She sets the galaxies a whirling. Love throughout it all. Seems she gave me a mighty heart not afraid to die, only just scared to find love or cry. Went out searching for what I was in this pie. Turned love away cause it once had hurt me, made me cry. So, what's left, SHE? What answer would you give me? My drama from the little me not worth much more than a bucket of goat pee. Spiritually turned here and there. Done things people would think is crazier than frog's hair. Words in this ornery fashion--Yes, at you I now am lashin'. Take me up or slam me down. What is all this clowning around? Time to take another step. Tried to understand and only wept, knowing that I Love you without knowing what that means. Sacred feminine, LOVE that is, take my heart. For you it truly is.

LEAP

Leap of heart over mind Love will change and leave now behind. The beginning was what it was, and then will be around the bend. The time is when none will know as many the Soothe has lied the truth. The Love will change as it must for life is Love so robust. So, the story must always never be for what is life other than imagined reality. So, the heart and soul will be Loves always goal and you are the story told, so, pray ye be bold.

MUDDIED

The Light and the Love, the stream of Joy, Wisdom. These are things that, perhaps, I have touched briefly, and pine for again with my mind, for I forget not their heavenly tastes. But alas, the mind is not the path to any of these, and my soul is so young. No guide have I. For what teacher would be with such as I? My path is muddied, and little this night is clear, except for the vision of the stars where I long to lie.

Weary Soul

There is Light even in the night, for darkness lurks in my worn and weary soul. The Light should be inside out, for that is what Love's Light is all about. My search is what it is and time cannot tell, for yesterday, maybe today. So now, intensely, I relax and let it be. For the Light is the Love you see.

Narcissists' Egos

Where are we? What are we? Am I one or three? Once I was a molecule, then a tool, perhaps a fool? The dream to be what one's mind does see interpreted by holy narcissists' egos flee. The dream of something, someone else, are things we will never be, in this reality. So, the where and what stew in a Goddess's pot, souls already know the plot driven by the circular symmetry of a single dot. So, I know only to cry out to all that was. So what? So fucking what? Will I never understand even a little part of the art of not?

Reflection

There is reflection, it is me, making me real and unreal at the same moment, I chose the wave until again I enter the ocean. Love gave me a heart to lend itself through to all that it may. I send balance and Love to all within its reach which be infinity. For as there is no then or to be there is no here or there.

SECRET

My life is secret. It should not be. All that glows in me should be for others to do with as they wish. My words seldom make sense. My soul is Love and not words, yet words are what everyone wants. The Love in me wants to be yours. The fear blocks this flow. The Love can win, but will I let it? I am yours, world. Do with me as you will, for I do not own, but only Love. It is true, but you do not know, for my life is a secret.

PEACE OUT

Beware the one who has just begun to be inside out and love’s all about, sometimes deeply in doubt, sometimes about to shout. Love's light is what it's about, not evil or death, but only the breath. Close your eyes and take that breath, for the rest is very much in doubt. Peace out!

HALF

I am half unbelievable story that is more than any can imagine and half rooted in reality so deeply that I live under the tree. Which, oh witch, is me? Will the magic carry me away or will the root grow troublesome upon me? Lordy, I must be what is turning into me, story, root and ego three. Only sanity is not the life for me. For soul is the universe and me - time to sleep and live in the clouds and under the sea. Lordy what a pickle I will in someday be.

BILLIE'S REALITY

What is this one reality? Why, for me it seems to be duality. Female and male am I. It's hard to explain just why. Spirituality and vanity, these two sometimes border me on insanity. Sorrow and joy, wolf and panther make me wonder what is the answer. God is three or God is one? Outside or in? How was all this begun? When the one reality does come, am I too much two? I am Love, and I am Fear. When the time comes, will I be here or will I disappear? To Love I do adhere, but doubt chases it over there, or is it over here? What is this one reality? Can I survive and Love even in my duality?

BRANCH 8

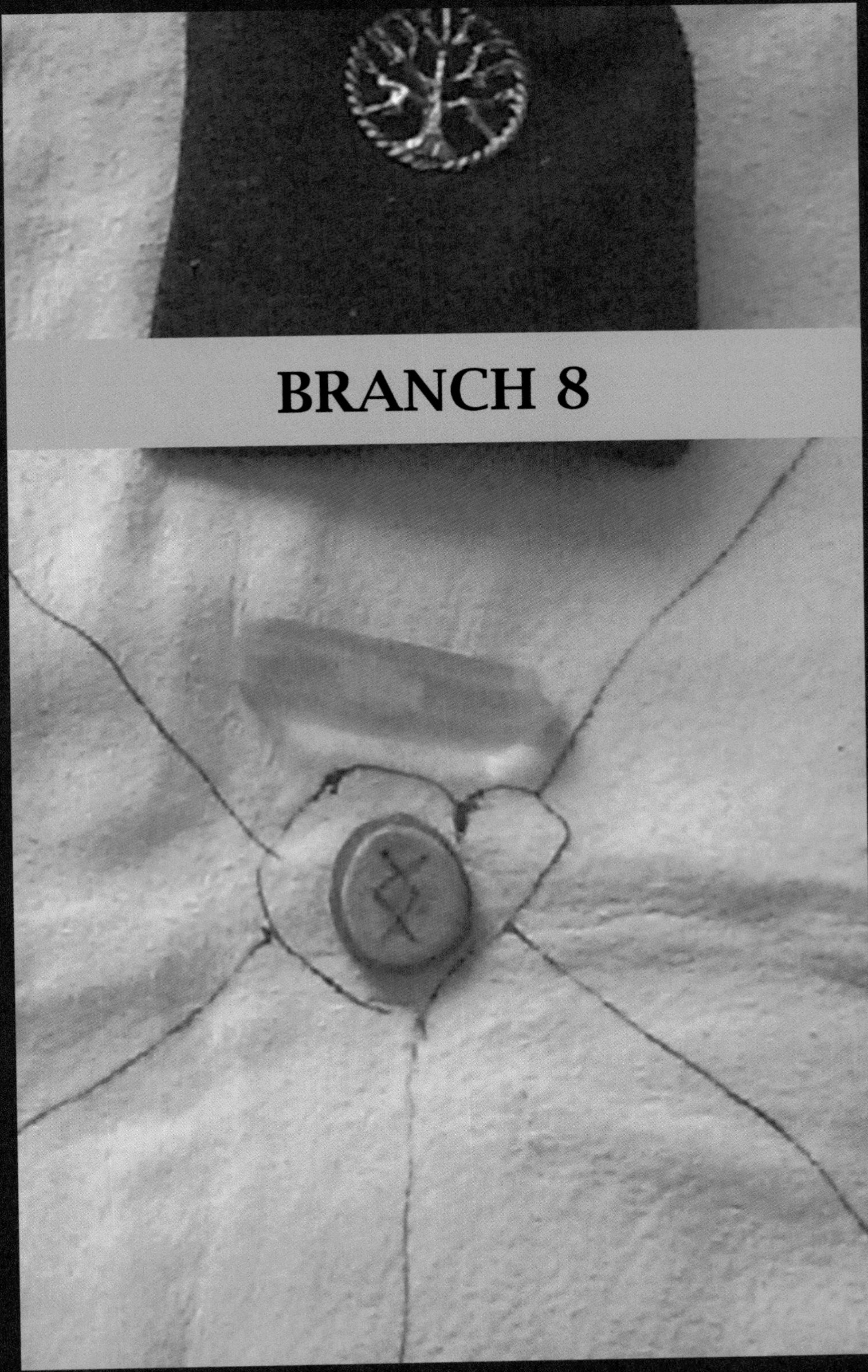

My Girl

My girl was hidden deep inside, buried by beer and shame. My girl appeared one day when the alcohol went away. My girl could not share for the shame; fear and pain were still in the game. My girl was discovered and burst upon the scene. My girl became my sister and had her day, and felt the light. My girl had a name and wanted to hear it said aloud. My girl is me, and I am she. Two parts my girl, Billie Sage, and me. My girl and me we are now whole. God willing, we will be happy and sane as my girl is me.

Through Your Eyes

A friend asked that I see me through your eyes and own this day. This is my attempt at that. I have changed in so many ways that even I am amazed at the light in my eyes sometimes, for that is what you see. You see that my soul has awakened and lives now where maybe it did not in the past. Yes, I put on makeup and a pretty scarf - But my heart is what is light and unwrinkled now, the place my soul resides awakens to the ethereal that is returning to the magic and the mystery that Love has always given us and that mankind has hidden. Oh, I still have plenty of growing and learning left to do, but I am closer now, too ready for the final judgment (which has nothing to do with hell and damnation) but rather is the time when all is seen as it truly is and when you reach the final judgment your heart will weigh like that of a feather and Love will be what you are. So, I take to HEART that I AM and that all of you are too, and like the days when I first started writing here (the days when I thought I was crazy but was really closer to truth) I say Love is all that is and ever has been, Love is the Alpha and Omega and is what holds this wave in place for you to play in. So, let Love into your heart and then let Love shine out to all that you see. BE Love and BE Peace. For in the end Love is all that matters in that YOU are never ending. Peace and Love, I pray this day that I may love as you have loved me and that we shall all be guided to the Peace within.

Desert Heart

Heal my heart upon its new start, kiss the Bard make her cry, Love never needs a why. Travel the path, twists and turns only in wisdom does she learn. When Spirit says to play all her worries go away. Bard on her knees, only souls beginning does she need to please. Wind in her ear, Love in her Desert Heart.

SCARY FAIRY

Sing a song of Love. The light guides from above. Never did I mean to be scary. I only wished I could be a flowing, beautiful fairy. When Love's Rose is reduced to the wave that we are, I can be reduced to the wave of a fairy on Love's star. The ways of the world confuse and belittle me, but always Love's Rose is truly real, when reduced to the wave that we all are. Love will always carry the Rose and I on the star. I cry because change is there for I and the rose, but always Love is there. The Light bends, but is always straight when a wave or a particle. Love will always be the real article. I always assume that Love I do wrong, but to the Light the Love and the Rose I always belong.

Religions

Oh holy night, when nevermore do religions live to fight! Love of freedom standing there, with Love in their eyes and Peace alive in their hearts. Oh holy night, when angels walk as man and man is forever angel's flight. Love is life, and Peace is reality when man understands the One morality. Oh holy night, when duality is flame's totality. I hear the angels. They say they are not but you a moment from now, when Love cries from your heart and joy flows from your eyes.

THE CHANGE

The time of change draws near, and others fear, but no longer do I. My heart is deep, and my mind is still, and what is before me is the Light's will, and I will not be harmed by the ones who do not understand. My love is still not released, but that too shall come when my time left in this body is as it should be. And my power will be what it should be, and my love will run deep for all those that want it of me. For I will not deny any who ask, and will love others as well, even unto my death.... For there is nothing else that matters to the universe except this love. Mine is not to know why. Mine is to search until I die, and when my earthly body lies still, my energy will be free, and those who hate will no longer harm me. As it is with all that are born to this life, whether they accept it or not, this life is but a looking glass and not the realness of Love in its true form.

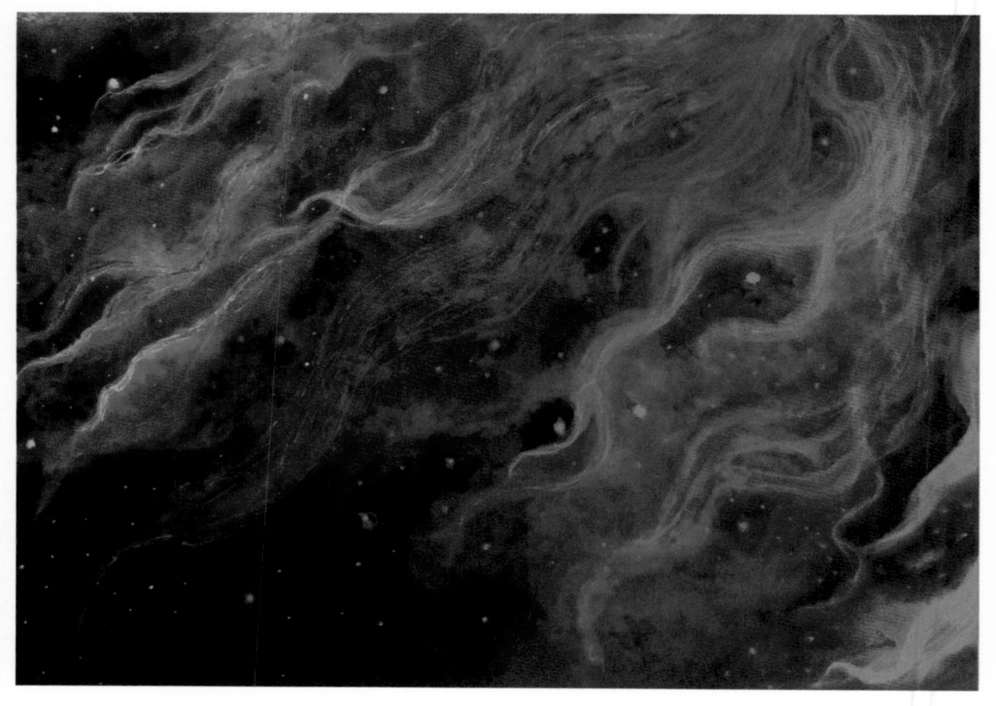

WHO AM I?

Humbly I ask, Who Am I? I am the bat and the mosquito, I am the puppy chasing its tail, I am the earth and the sky, I am the flower and the butterfly, I am the bee and the honey, I am the daughter and the soul and I am the star and its light. Humbly I ask, who am I? I AM and I am is Love.

Merry Child

When did you know that a snowflake was the most fabulous art? When did you ride the sun and fill the moon in your heart? When was the adventure more than all the universe from finish to start? Why when you were young of course, when you were a child all love was intense and never mild. You would kiss an alligator and ride a bunny wild. You could eat the heavens and burp strawberries from light until dark. The days were long and the trees would sway and sing you their song while you did play. So now, I say, to you this time of year, again you must let the child be your biggest part. Let the tears grow the flowers of spring, let the grin go from your forehead to your chin. If you do these things, let the child within be your guide. The universe will give you oh such a ride, you will be star shine and Love on the inside. So, Merry Child to you and cheers to your Love of the new year.

Silvery Tone

I watch the stars float slowly by and wonder what it feels like to no longer cry, the weary tears of so many of history's years. The race ran for who knows how long a span, the memory of Love in every wrinkled tan. This we know in every way, some say Love does never go away, but time may take the flesh and bone and only leave the flutes silvery tone. Then what memory will the universe hand the new that never knew this Love filled land? Perhaps it will send all the love and tears of so many years through the news very ears. For when Love is in the ears bone, all that was will be in every flutes silvery tone.

THE SHIP

"The future is yours to write," the old fortune teller had said. And so, in the quiet of the morning, I got out my pen, and I wrote… and as I wrote I began to float the soul entered a 20-mast boat, so I sailed the star filled sea and wandered through out eternity. Where I went I saw such wonders purple love and beings with jelly eyes you can only imagine my surprise. The ship took me to places not yet, some so dry with my saddest memory I could not cry, some so wet I have water in my ears even yet. I float and sailed and wrote letters and gave them to beaver bears to be mailed. The day wore on and became night a billion years I sailed in one moments light. And as I sailed eternity I understood a single thing, the world without love doesn't mean a thing. So, I wrote that in my heart and guided my ship back into never start knowing now that with love in this world I can only do my loving part.

Me at Last

The dark road now is past. Life then was shadow. Life then was death, liquor my only friend. Knowing that inside never matched out, wondering what I was all about. Hate from 6 to 49, hate of me from sea to pine. Learned to be the man they wanted, the girl I am never flaunted. Then the choice to live or die, darkness or light, wallow or fly. Let Billie out. Let Billie try. Follow the light. Learn from earth and sky. Love is what matters, the inside is now the same as out, learning what life is about. The road ahead is the Light. Billie's choice now: Love and flight. Now from darkness to Light, the dark road is now long past. I look up and ask, am I now free? Free to be me at last?

Cedar Tree

Wild thoughts of winter's bane. Living hearts with love's sane. Give the darkness. Walk in the light. Infinity shows its heavy might. Caring eyes that see past the mask. Love of Boo is all I ask. Holy heights, moment's depth. Wild thoughts of Summer rains. In this world, I must walk in the sand over burning rock. When the Moon the Goddess sky weaves the Love and makes eyes cry, leaves a heart that wonders why. Soul is alone on this plane. Kiss the bane, and wash in rain. Love in heart, and set aside that which is brain. While I weave some words of wood, my spirit still now where ALL once stood. Come the seasons of what BE. One is I, and all is three. For LOVE sent me the Cedar tree.

No Doubt

In the sky, a bumble bee does fly, even though the scientist cannot see why, no doubt. When a caterpillar goes inside its house, it comes out a butterfly, even though a human asks why, no doubt. A mountain Jesus said you could move with something the size of a mustard seed, no doubt. When Buddha said peace was inside, there seemed to be a glow about, no doubt. Love makes life exist with impossible odds, no doubt. The human heart will change the world to Love and Peace when they do decide, no doubt. Who has the light inside that can shine it out? You, no doubt.

DID YOU?

Did you watch every beautiful sunrise and sunset? Did you look deeply into the eyes of the one you love until there was no you beginning and their ending? Did you breathe in the stars and exhale the sun? Did you dance with the Goddess in the pale moonlight? Did you tell Mother that you love her for letting you have this ride? Did you even once question who you are? Did you cry until there was no salt left in your veins? Did you laugh until your mirth rode the lighting in the sky? Did you know you will never die? Did you turn your fear away and choose Love one moment of one day? Did you dance in the star sand and hold God's hand? Did I? Perhaps some not all said I, but the others I will surely try.

BRANCH 9

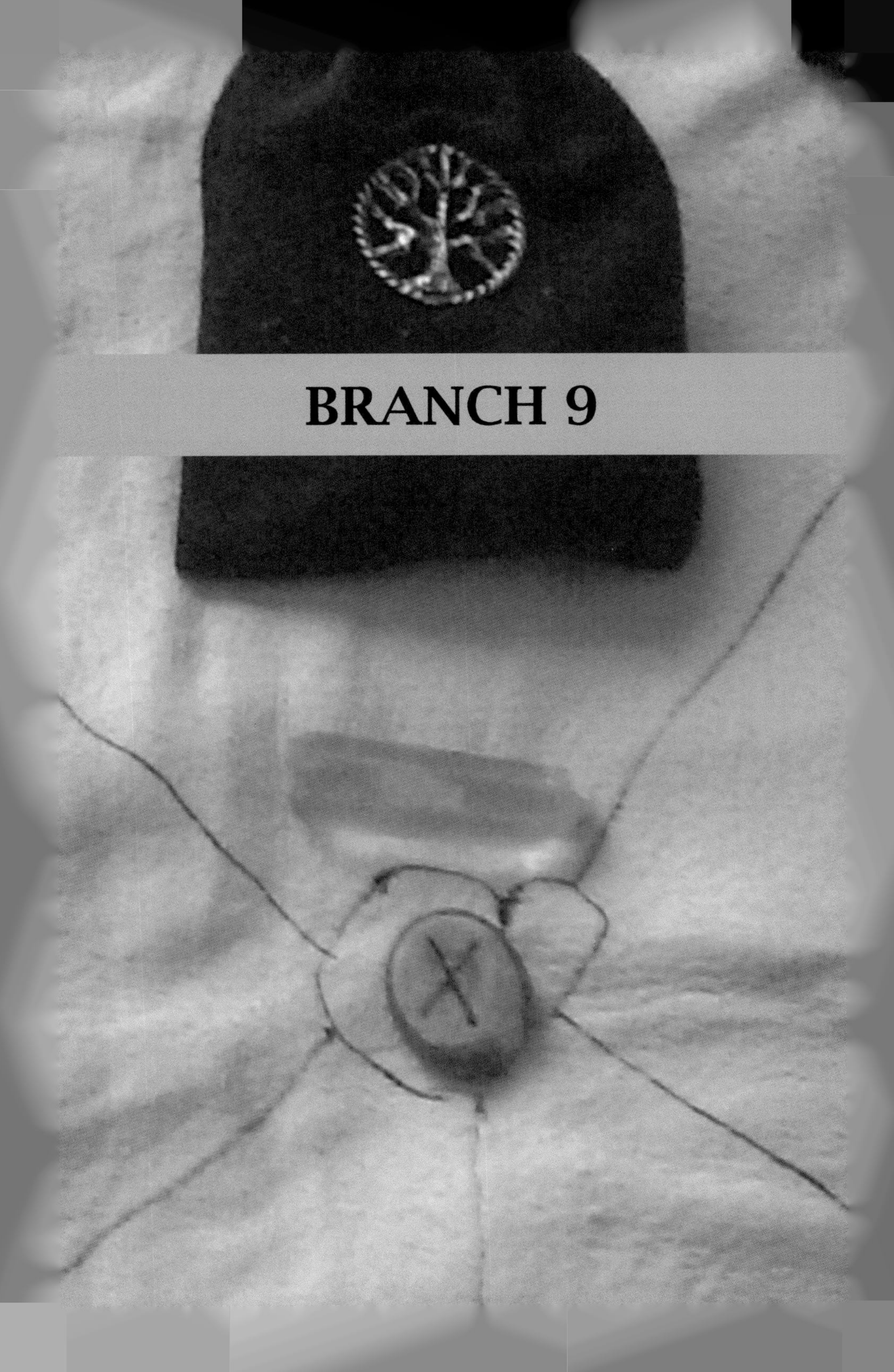

STATUS QUO

Status quo is what you know, but you should know that you do not know, so, you look above and below, but soon you find this is not where you need to go. So, look inside and you begin to find that the answer that is there is no status quo, and, oh, you find you really do not know other than what you know. So now we let this that we are be, and, oh, my you find Love is what IS and IS what Love you be. And there you go. Now you know that you do not know, so just let life flow and BE Love as you go.

FRIEND

The Light leads me forward; on in life I go. The Love gives me friends so I may grow. They know not the seeds they sow. Fore they give my soul a chance to glow. Pretty you are, they say. My eyes show me a different way. You are fine as you are. My soul still wishes upon a star. My path still winds on. My soul still needs to grow. My skin is still not complete. My soul still seeks to glow. The Light is steady forever always. The friends, ever there for love. My skin still uncomfortable. My soul still able to grow. The light shall always shine. The Love will always give. The seeds will always grow. The soul is still unknown. The friend is the Love. The friend is with the Light. The friend encourages me to grow. The friend touches my soul.

-- Dedicated to Jan

Never Alone

I have been stone, star and bone. I have died hero, slave and gnome. Warrior, Goddess and Witch each time another stitch. Turn the bone, roll the stone, listen to star lights tone. Deep within everywhere and everything I have been. Burn the blood; cast the rune dance naked in the darkness of the new moon. Crawl from the cave, slither in the dust listen to the cry of the loon. Kiss and Cry, Live or Die empty hole scream at the sky. Love tells me it's not new, live the life marked in blue every moment I swear is a dart of Heart to Boo. Between the lines, scratch the dirt, battered and bruised, Peace is never confused. Kiss the wood, hold the stone, never in Love am I alone.

The One I Feed

I sing to the sky for the moon is God in my eye, some would call it a cry but it only sounds lonely because my soul is made to fly. The sound is long and luminous, on the wind is harmonious like a hug from inside universal continuous. When the sound begins to die one may only wipe the moisture from thine eye for the sound has brought infinity into a short sigh. The lone wolf is what is on my mind, for it is my true heart and the one that I feed is indeed growing in Love's Light from the start.

Boo

Boo was my dog she loved me unconditionally, dog spelled the other way is god, Boo is my god for she was good, and taught what church could not. Love is and heaven was, 'tis truth when the story is told. Believe in only the now is folly for you are I and we BE very old.

Can I Say?

Can I say something to you? Even if it or I upset you? You are part of me, and I am part of you. If this is true, then is not Love more important than what we own? For really, what do you own? When you and I depart after our measly 80 years or so, what will you take? Your land? Your money? I hope I take my love and my soul, and where I go that these I still may share. We will all be there, you a part of me, me a part of you. Is it okay these things I say? Can I say I love, or will you run away?

Moon's Mountains Sky

Clouds! Dark giant mountains. One spear of moonlight break. Anticipation! Vision's next, eyes wide watch. Glowing dome! Climb out of mountains dark heights. Moon! The giant now fills and lights cloud mountains once dark sky. Wonder! Always fills you inside. O beauty! Of moon goddess sky. Splendor! When from behind dark cloud mountains you did arise. Love! Of such beauty fills heart and eye.

WALKING THE PATH

Walking, walking we three: Bonnie, the Light, and me. Walking the path, the path with thee. Walking, listening, seeing each thing anew. Walking to see and be three Bonnie, I, and You. Talking to learn and understand, Bonnie and I. You, as always, silent, there to guide if we let thee. Walking, and now a vision of you. Stop and look, a tear for your Beauty, the hug inside. Walking back the path, your buzzing made us flee. Walking the path hurry, hurry man's machine, move now! Walking again, your guide heeded, we listen to thee. Walk, slow now, stop and look I say. The Light, glorious to view having gotten to the perfect spot. The spot where you wanted Bonnie and I to be with You. The Beauty the Hug inside, no words can tell. A tear, a sigh, a silent thanks to you. Walking the path, the path with thee. Walking, walking we three Bonnie, the Light, and me.

-- With all my love for Bonnie.
It came in my dream
and was time to be written.

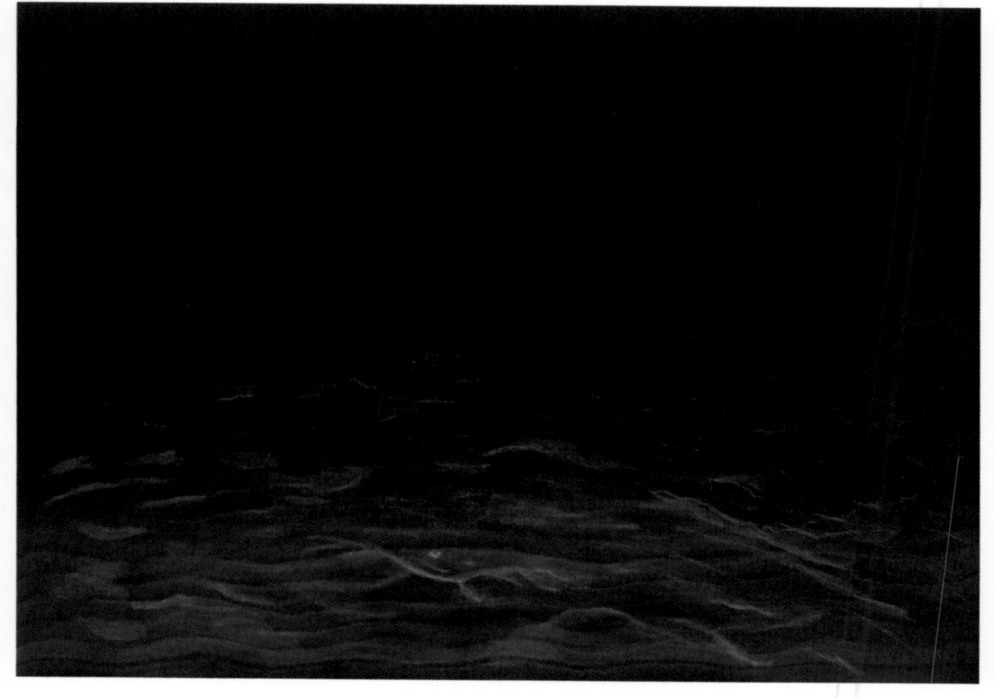

GIFT

The crow's caw. The sky glows red. The puppies bark. The sky, like a red glowing spark. The pigeon on the wire. What does it bring, that sky fire? The air is so still, and the glow begins to fade. The sun goes down. The beauty is not this moment but that. Now, slightly gray sunset made me feel a certain way. Life is a wonderful gift in many a way.

THE RIDE

Two souls out for a ride sit in a car side by side quiet most of the time. What do they feel inside? Two souls out for a ride thinking there is much pain to hide: One the pain of loss, one the pain of fear. Two souls who sometimes cry. Two souls enjoy Gods beauty stop to picture a little of solid reality. Two souls stop to listen. The Light sends them a whisper of wind up the valley, one moment of peaceful spirituality. The ride back to human reality. Two souls with pain to hide sit quietly side by side enjoying the day's ride

-- For Jan, with all my love

PATHS

There are many paths, and you must choose. That is the truth of the Love, you can choose. Fear of death makes it easy to allow others to choose for you. Life wants to exist, Love makes this so. If you allow others to choose for you, you give up what Love gave you. You are part of everything. Everything is sacred. You are sacred. Be Love. Leave the fear to the dark where it should reside. Be the Light that you are, Love always inside.

#NODAPL

Sleepless before I go, hours pass like molasses. On the road 14 hours turns to 20, no problems other than police in Belle Fourche. Sleepless as I drive or ride, close, so many deer on the road side. Arrive, many religious groups here to help water protectors survive. Stand and listen to so many blow their wind, important words sure. Standing in prayer staring at the police in military gear, why? The water protectors, the religions, hundreds of people this day. Hopeful that our hearts were heard and the black snake will go away. Finally, 36 hours awake, asleep in the tent on the ground in Oceti Sakowin. Next day feel the prayers, watch and listen, learn. Pray in my own way. Help do camp dishes, meet smiling wonderful people from many places. Listen, smell, hear, feel the prayers of so many in the camp. Impacts me deeply I will never forget, I will cry when I remember sometimes. This is how to live, together, as people, messy but alive and respectful of all. Be there I ask of all of you, if not in person, then in prayer. Help stop the Black Snake. Take your fear out of your heart and listen to what Mother must say. Water is Life, oil is death, listen with your heart. So, that all of us will have another day to watch children play.

Still, But Not Last

I twist and turn in the wind, gentle waving riding your eternity. I wish to grow callous, but you let me not. I sway and wail and dance the dervish, trying to let darkness prevail. But Love, you tell me again, that is what there is not sin. My electrons I wish to wander free, and still only Love you are there for me. Holding in my sanity the glue of life, Love you send to me. The tears are not shame. No, sin is not to blame. But only Love is thy true game. For when we fall from the future and leave no past, that is when the circle is complete and again we are Love .... at last.

The Same

Wonders, wanders, withers, and wanes, wants to feel life with her heart instead of her brains. Up, down, in, and out, wants to know what Love is really about. Sly, shy, witty, and cry, wants to find her wings and fly. Wolf, cat, owl, and bat, wants to know where the answers are at. Hear, feel, taste, and see, we are all the same you and me.

Triad Rune

Printed in Great Britain
by Amazon